DUMPLINGS EQUAL LOVE

DUMP

DELICIOUS RECIPES FROM AROUND THE WORLD

LINGS
LOVE

Liz Crain

PHOTOGRAPHY BY
Dina Avila

SASQUATCH BOOKS
SEATTLE

CONTENTS

RECIPE LIST

MORIMOTO

KOREATOWN

TORO BRAVO

JOHN GORHAM & LIZ CRAIN

DUMPLINGS

=

THE FRENCH LAUNDRY COOKBOOK THOMAS KELLER

ESSENTIAL **PEPIN** JACQUES PÉPIN

The Joy

A New Generation of JOY

NGUYEN

CHUN

NGUYEN

KATZ

Bittman

JaPa

Katz

Sándor Ellix Kat

INTRODUCTION

I was nine or ten years old the first time I had dumplings. My family was out to dinner at a Chinese restaurant not far from downtown Cincinnati, owned and run by a Chinese family. Our server, the restaurant owner's son, who was in his late teens and always dressed in a fresh-pressed, immaculate black suit, smiled as he set the dumplings down in the middle of our table. He actually bowed to them. Then, with one hand behind his back, he lifted the steamer lid and a plume of savory, Chinese-chives-spiked steam wafted up toward our noses. I knew that food would never be the same for me again.

Every time we ate at that restaurant after that first bamboo steamer tray of *shumai*, and we ate there often, I hoped that our order would include them. It usually did, although sometimes spring rolls won out.

When Sasquatch Books asked me to write this cookbook, during a meal at the Portland Book Festival in 2018 where we unsurprisingly shared dumplings, this memory and others lit up for me, one after the other, like a meteor shower—the vegetarian Chinese *su jiao* dumplings I learned to make in my early twenties with my friend Raquel; the hundreds of thick-skinned pan-fried dumplings that I ate throughout college at the small just-off-campus counter-service Chinese restaurant; my first steamy platter of buttery potato pierogi at Portland's annual Polish Festival;

the mind-expanding array of beautiful shrimp and pork dumplings I ate as a child while traveling throughout Asia with my travel-agent grandma; my first brothy, pleated Chinese *xiao long bao* that I hunted down in Seattle and was unsure how exactly to eat.

Most cultures claim and celebrate some sort of dumpling, regardless of what your definition of *dumpling* is—and there are *many*. Historically, dumplings have been small, hand-filled, bite-size treats enjoyed morning, noon, and night. They are often made at home and with meager ingredients, and they are usually steeped in regional and familial stories.

I sourced many of the traditional, and beloved worldwide, dumplings in this book directly from friends and loved ones whose families hold these recipes dear and have passed them from generation to generation, such as the Korean pork and kimchi *mandu*, Japanese *gyoza*, and sour pickle pierogi. Other recipes were inspired by my family, my travels, and my home kitchen, such as the Cincinnati chili, shrimp and grits, bananas Foster, and nettle dumplings. *All* the dumplings in this cookbook are rooted in deep cultural respect, steeped in my own personal curiosity, and fed by a lot of nose-in-old-cookbooks research. I enjoyed immersing myself in the history and culture of many of the dishes and dumplings in these pages as much as I did developing the recipes.

To me, dumplings equal love no matter what culture they come from or how they are cooked. They are the food that I often crave when I'm under the weather or my head hangs low. And they are the food that I want to cook for loved ones when they are going through a rough spell. I've always carried a torch for hidden foods, the heart of the matter all steamy, aromatic, and nestled inside, waiting

to comfort those who eat them. When you take a tender dumpling skin, fill it with deliciousness, and hand-form it, you are ensuring that every bite counts, that every moment matters.

This cookbook is at once a message of love via dumplings and a celebration of culinary diversity. *Dumplings Equal Love* includes more than twenty traditional and not-so-traditional dumpling recipes from around the world. In these pages, you'll find recipes for everything from hearty, fist-sized, grated-potato-and-barley-flour Norwegian *komper*, and those small, delicate Chinese shumai, to Pacific Northwest morel dumplings in orange-hued, smoky pimenton skins. There are also recipes for everything from dumpling doughs that you can enhance with vibrant powdered vegetables, fruits, and spices, to versatile dipping sauces and workhorse pantry staples.

Mass-market, industrialized food lies on one end of the spectrum, dumplings decidedly on the other. No two homemade dumplings are ever exactly the same, and they're often as strikingly beautiful as they are delicious. I love that, internationally, dumplings have always straddled the dual roles of inexpensive, and often familial, comfort food and ceremonial, celebratory festival and holiday food. Whether dumplings were delivered in a parade of platters at imperial Chinese banquets during China's more than two thousand years of emperor rule, or filled with healing herbs and boiled up over an outdoor fire to treat frostbite and illness, they have always provided us with regionalism in an ever-globalizing world. Their stories and flavors help us understand ourselves and others.

I want to be very clear from page one that store-bought dumpling skins are perfectly acceptable for most dumplings in this book. In fact, they're often my go-to.

When you're feeling pulled in too many directions, sad, or just plain out of sorts, popping into the store for a tiny parcel of dumpling skins, and then whipping up a small bowl of filling once home, is sometimes all that's needed to get things back on a manageable track. You fill the skins, form the dumplings, set them in a boiling pot, hot oiled pan, or bamboo steamer, and know that in less than fifteen minutes everything will feel a whole lot better—bite after steamy bite. It's a simple way to take sweet care of yourself and loved ones.

I can't tell you how often people tell me that they would love to make dumplings from scratch, but it's just too time-consuming and tedious. It doesn't have to be, and I'll go so far as to say that, in general, it should not be. One of my greatest goals with this book is to help you not just make but enjoy making dumplings from start to finish—skins and all.

I want to take the strain out of the process, to set you up for dumpling-making success with advice on sequencing tasks, as well as tips and tools for streamlining everything. If you, like me, often turn to simple kitchen projects to make things right in your world, to either soften its edges or celebrate the small stuff, you'll find a friend in this book.

Dumplings don't ask for much. All they require is a series of small tasks, nothing too complicated or technique driven, nothing too particular. When you set into making a batch the path-of-least-resistance way—the *Dumplings Equal Love* way—your mind and body ease up a bit, as you move into the straightforward tasks of chopping and mincing, seasoning and stirring, forming and cooking, and finally, thank goodness, eating. Dumplings equal love.

GETTING STARTED

As much as I love to travel and cook in other kitchens, I most likely will not be in yours when you make these dumplings. So here are a few guiding principles that I would lead by example with, that will make the endeavor more enjoyable and eliminate potential pitfalls.

No Store-Bought Shame!

Buying and using store-bought dumpling skins is perfectly acceptable. I do it all the time. They're cheap and tasty, often easy to source in grocery stores and Asian markets in small refrigerated or frozen packages, and they can greatly reduce the amount of time it takes to make dumplings at home. Typically you'll have a choice between square wonton wrappers (which you can always trim into a circular skin) and round gyoza or dumpling skins. Sometimes you'll even get a choice of thin or thick dumpling skins. Although it's entirely up to you, I generally prefer thin skins for my dumplings.

All of that said, I recommend trying your hand at homemade dough at least once. Homemade skins are significantly more pliable, workable, and easy to seal than store-bought, and they usually result in more fetching dumplings. They also have better bite and flavor, and you can make them with all sorts of colorful herbs, spices, and powdered vegetables and fruits (see page 52).

Keep It All Covered

Always cover formed skins and dumplings with a dry towel so that they don't lose or gain moisture. Dumpling dough dries up surprisingly quickly when exposed to air, making it difficult to handle and cook. If it's particularly humid, or if you are doing a lot of steaming or boiling nearby, uncovered dough can also gather moisture and get sticky.

Underfill to Start

It is frustrating when dumpling filling erupts out of the top of a dumpling like a volcano as you're forming it. Underfill to start and work your way up to plumper, full-bellied dumplings.

Lightly Flour *Everything*

Always place formed and uncooked dumplings on a lightly floured work surface, baking sheet or platter, piece of parchment or waxed paper, or silicone mat so that they don't stick. Ditto for dumpling skins and doughs. If it's uncooked, made of dough, and in the kitchen, keep it on a lightly floured surface.

Either cook formed dumplings right away, or cover and refrigerate them for up to three hours before cooking. XLB dumplings (see page 92) are the exception and should be either cooked or frozen immediately.

Most dumplings freeze incredibly well, unless they are potato or egg filled. You simply cook them straight from frozen, generally adding two to three minutes to the cook time.

To freeze, place them on a lightly floured baking sheet or platter (if you like, top it with parchment or waxed paper, or a silicone mat, lightly floured) so that none are touching, for one to two hours, until the dumplings are frozen. I usually use a thin, aluminum pizza tray that fits perfectly in my chronically overfull, tiny freezer.

Once frozen, nudge the dumplings off the sheet or platter (or knock the bottom of it onto a table or work surface to quickly loosen them), being careful not to rip the bottoms. Then dust off any clinging flour and seal them in a freezer bag with as little air as possible. For most dumplings in this book, you can fit fifteen to twenty in a quart freezer bag and sixty to eighty in a gallon size. Always label bags clearly with the date that you made them, along with the filling and dough type. Your future self will thank you. Freeze dumplings for up to one month.

I usually take frozen dumpling bags out of the freezer once, several hours after initially putting them in, and give them a good jostle to make sure that no dumplings are sticking together. Then I let them seriously *chill*. Sorry, bad joke.

It's pretty sweet to have a variety of homemade dumplings ready and waiting in your freezer. While I was working on this book, I had an average of twenty to thirty different types of dumplings in mine. That means that in ten to twenty minutes I could whip up a yummy, diverse dumpling meal for me and hungry loved ones. I plan to always have a freezer full—well, partially full—of dumplings from this day forward.

TEST COOKING

It's a good idea to cook off a test patty of filling before forming dumplings. This is your chance to get an overall feel for the flavor, texture, and juiciness of the future dumplings.

You want dumpling filling to be slightly more salty, spiced, and flavorful than it should be if served on its own, since it will ultimately be cloaked in what amounts to a wide noodle. Think of dumpling fillings in the same way that you think of robust sauces for pasta.

To test the filling, preheat a small skillet with one teaspoon of vegetable oil over medium-low heat for one to two minutes. Form one tablespoon of dumpling filling into a small patty, and cook it in the pan for three to four minutes. Flip it once about halfway through. Remove it from the pan, and once it has cooled a bit, try it. If something isn't quite to your liking, now is the time to adjust.

If the filling is too loose to form a patty, or is for XLB, fill a steaming pot one-quarter to half full with water, and bring it to a boil over high heat. Put one tablespoon or so of the loose filling in a flat Asian soup spoon, tartlet mold, or other small, open, heatproof holder, and place it in the steamer. Steam the filling for six to seven minutes.

I also recommend forming and cooking one dumpling before forming them all, to test steaming, pan-frying, or boiling. After cooking a test dumpling, you can make any necessary adjustments to the bigger batch in terms of form, cook time, and technique. You can even form three and try steaming, pan-frying, *and* boiling to see which results in the best taste, texture, and overall delicious dumpling experience. The results often surprise me.

THE RIGHT TOOLS

While in the thick of recipe testing for this book, I sustained a tennis injury that began in my arm and put me out of kitchen commission for a few weeks. During that time, I regretted how physical dumpling making can be. The silver lining is that it pushed me to find work-arounds, less physically demanding ways to handle dumpling dough that I can now share with you.

Of course, one way to quickly reduce physical labor is to use store-bought dumpling skins. There are also a lot of handy-dandy tools. For example, a food processor or stand mixer (my preferred method) make dough mixing and kneading much faster and easier.

If you have a stand mixer, I highly recommend using a mechanical pasta-roller attachment for rolling out the dough sheets. A much cheaper hand-crank pasta roller is helpful as well, but naturally requires more elbow grease. You can also use a dumpling maker to quickly shape dumplings.

What follows is a slew of tools I love that will come in handy in your dumpling kitchen.

ASIAN SOUP SPOONS—I steam and serve XLB in lightly oiled, heatproof stainless-steel or ceramic Asian soup spoons, placed head to toe in the steamer. I also like tartlet molds for this purpose (see page 13). Asian soup spoons are deep, flat bottomed, short handled, and fun to eat with. Dumplings are often juicy, especially XLB, so it's nice to use chopsticks to eat them from (and over) an Asian soup spoon. That way you don't lose any yummy broth!

BAMBOO DUMPLING TONGS—These handsome tools come in handy for cooking and serving dumplings. They are slender, rounded, and nonstick (dumpling skin can be tacky) and come in all different sizes. My favorites are nine inches long.

BAMBOO SPREADERS—I really dig my six- to eight-inch, flat, nonstick spreaders, also known as wooden butter knives or cheese spreaders. They work wonders with scooping up and spreading tacky dumpling fillings (filling often gets stuck in spoons) onto dumpling skins, and they are affordable and durable. Multipacks are usually less than ten dollars.

BAMBOO STEAMERS—Beautiful tiered, woven bamboo steamers are one of my favorite pieces of kitchen equipment. Watch for them at thrift stores, estate sales, et cetera, because new ones can cost a pretty penny. Metal steamers aren't as handsome as bamboo ones, and they also gather quite a bit of moisture at the top that drips onto the dumplings. Bamboo steamers are usually four, eight, ten, twelve, or fourteen inches in diameter, and stainless-steel-banded

BAMBOO SPREADERS

PASTRY CUTTER

DOWEL ROLLING PINS

DUMPLING MAKER

COOKIE CUTTERS

TARTLET MOLDS

BAMBOO STEAMER

BAMBOO DUMPLING TONGS

ASIAN SOUP SPOONS

PASTRY/BENCH SCRAPER

ones are very durable. I think eight-inch steamers are the most practical since most kitchens have an eight-inch-diameter pot, and each layer holds eight to ten dumplings. The four-inch steamers are pretty stinking cute—kids get a kick out of them—and twelve- and fourteen-inch ones work well for parties. *All* sizes are lovely for steaming and reheating all sorts of food, including veggies, fish, and shellfish.

BISCUIT OR COOKIE CUTTERS—In general, for dumpling skins I recommend three-, three-and-a-half-, and four-inch cutters with handles. I often use an overturned metal cocktail shaker too (most are three and a half inches in diameter), which is handy since many kitchens have one.

CHEESECLOTH, NYLON MESH BREWING/STRAINING BAGS, OR THIN CHEF TOWELS—Any of these work like a charm for squeezing out moist ingredients. I regularly use nylon mesh brewing bags (each ten dollars or less) for everything from squeezing grated potato to straining fruit wines. After using, quickly rinse and hand- or machine wash.

CHOPSTICKS—These excellent dining utensils also come in handy for mixing doughs, filling dumplings, whisking eggs, and peeking at the bottoms of dumplings as they sizzle in the pan. Stainless-steel ones are well suited for cooking and are dishwasher safe.

DOWEL ROLLING PINS—Lightweight, handle-less, often tapered rolling pins are your friends when hand-rolling dumpling skins. They are easy to maneuver and work wonders with small pieces of dough. I use my twelve-inch bamboo dowel pin for individual skins and my twenty-inch maple for sheets. You can just use an old wine bottle instead! If you're making a lot of dumplings or hand-rolling lacks appeal, feed the dough through a manual or electric pasta roller for similar results.

DUMPLING MAKERS—These hinged metal or plastic gadgets are designed to form crimped crescent dumplings and often double as dumpling-skin cutters. I prefer to hand-form dumplings, but these do work. I was skeptical. If using one, underfill dumplings so they don't erupt, and make sure the skin size matches the gadget's diameter.

KITCHEN TIMERS—I always have at least one kitchen timer with the count-up feature, and magnetic timers are particularly handy. If I'm timing something in the fridge or freezer, I can stick one on the respective door, and if I'm timing the stovetop or oven, I put one on the hood. Have a few timers—less chance of mucking up your phone!

LAZY SUSANS—Load these up with dumplings and all sorts of dishes filled with tasty treats and dipping sauces, and give them a whirl. An eighteen-inch-diameter one is quite versatile since it can fit a couple of eight-inch steamer trays plus sides and sauces.

PASTA ROLLERS/SHEETERS—If you plan to make dumplings (or pasta) more than a handful of times, I recommend a hand-crank or electric pasta-roller machine or stand-mixer attachment, for ease plus speed when rolling out dough sheets. For stand-mixer attachments, you simply turn the mixer on, select your speed, and feed the dough through the roller. Many manual pasta machines also have electric motor attachments.

PASTRY/BENCH SCRAPER—In addition to cutting dough, these make quick work of dough and flour cleanup. Scrape your surface with it, brush it off with your hand or a dry towel, and then go in with a wet sponge or rag. If you start cleaning with the latter, you'll have a gluey mess. A scraper also deftly lifts sticky dough sheets from kitchen surfaces.

PASTRY CUTTER/WHEEL—This tool, used to cut shapes and lines in sheets of dough, can be either fluted (scalloped), straight, or double headed. If you want to make art skins (see page 56), get the latter.

REUSABLE PUMP BOTTLES—Rather than wasting steamer parchment paper (common in restaurants), I prefer oiling bamboo steamer trays, as well as pans and Asian soup spoons for XLB with easy-peasy spray oil. There are quite a few single-use, nonaerosol spray-oil products out there, but if you purchase a reusable pump bottle, you can fill it with your favorite oil. I recommend a translucent bottle so you can see what's inside and how much is left.

SMALL SPATULAS—I buy large packs of these rubber or silicone spatulas every few years and share them with friends. I like the six-inch size best. They come in handy when quickly transferring sauces from small bowls and ramekins, and scraping things out of small or oddly shaped jars and containers that larger spatulas can't nose their way into.

STEAMING POTS—If you don't have a steaming ring, use whatever thickest-rimmed pot is the same diameter as your steamer so that the steamer tray doesn't slip and slide. Any old pot will do, but squat pots are more efficient since you can use less water and heat to steam the dumplings. Steamers can also be placed in a wok to steam.

STEAMING RINGS—This flat aluminum or stainless-steel ring, with a seven-inch opening, converts many pots into steaming pots while protecting and stabilizing steamer baskets. The eleven-inch Helen Chen/Helen's Asian Kitchen steaming ring works for both eight-, ten-, and twelve-inch bamboo steamers. It gives you a few inches of leeway so that a slightly smaller or larger pot will work.

TARTLET MOLDS—Use reusable aluminum, stainless-steel, silicone, or ceramic tartlet molds for steaming and serving soup dumplings. I recommend ones with a two-inch base since that's the average diameter of XLB. I really like my fluted aluminum ones—they're durable, affordable, nonstick, and fit well in my steamer. They're cute too.

SPECIAL INGREDIENTS

Some of these ingredients will require visiting an Asian market or shopping online, and they are all used in multiple recipes in the book. If you aren't familiar with an ingredient here, or haven't used it before, I'm pretty sure it will open new doors to your home cooking.

AGAR-AGAR—Agar-agar, also sometimes referred to simply as *agar*, is an algae-derived gelatin alternative that's the secret to my XLB soup dumplings. Use powdered agar-agar if you can find it. Most Asian markets carry it in the flour and starch section; it's sometimes in the

CHINKIANG VINEGAR

GARLIC CHIVES

DRIED SHIITAKE MUSHROOMS

SICHUAN PEPPERCORNS

SHAOXING WINE

AGAR-AGAR

health-food section of conventional grocery stores, and you can always order it online. If you use flaked agar-agar, use about three times as much by volume. If you use agar-agar stick, chop it up and cook it for one to two minutes longer until fully dissolved. Do *not* use sweetened agar-agar powders in XLB.

BLACK AND ZHENJIANG/CHINKIANG VINEGARS—Zhenjiang, or Chinkiang, is a city in China's Jiangsu province known for its tart and slightly sweet black vinegar made from glutinous rice and malt. It's one of the most well-known and popular types of black vinegar worldwide. Most Chinese black vinegars—there are many different types and regional variations—are made from rice, wheat, millet, or sorghum, and they are a traditional and delicious accompaniment to XLB dumplings. Better black vinegars are well aged and have a smoky depth of flavor.

DRIED SHIITAKE OR BLACK MUSHROOMS—There are so many different types of dried "black mushrooms" (which are in fact shades of gray and brown), but almost all of them in American Asian markets are various grades and sizes of whole-cap or sliced dried shiitake. They're a yummy, versatile pantry ingredient and my go-to meat substitute for many recipes in this book. When shopping, use your best judgment by look and feel and, when in doubt, go for a mid- to higher-range shiitake. I love the chewy, meaty bite and woodsy flavor that reconstituted shiitakes add to dumplings.

GARLIC CHIVES/CHINESE CHIVES/*NIRA*—This perennial plant in the onion family has long, grasslike leaves that are more strongly flavored than the chives used in Western cooking. I like them in dumplings, ramen soups, deviled eggs, and salads, which is good because they often come in very large bunches. Flowering garlic chives are a particular delicacy if you can find them (or grow them!).

RICE VINEGAR—Some rice vinegar is made from rice that's been cooked and treated with yeast, while most is made from rice wine lees (the yeasty sediment produced during winemaking) and alcohol. Typically, rice vinegar is clear to golden in color and a bit sweeter and less acidic than other vinegars. You can make rice vinegar at home from rice wine and a vinegar culture (a.k.a. vinegar mother)—it's often a beautiful cloudy white, like coconut water, and delicious—but you don't have to go to such lengths. Give all vinegars a small, quick swig before using to see what you're working with.

CHEN PI: DRIED TANGERINE PEEL

Peel an organic tangerine or mandarin (since you'll be eating the skin) into several roughly 1-inch pieces. Don't worry about scraping off the pith—it adds flavor, nutrition, and a slight bitter balance. Set the pieces on a wire rack to air-dry in a sunny spot, as they do in China, for 3 or 4 days, until they curl a bit and become dry but still pliable. Once dry, store them in an airtight container for up to 2 months. Many believe that the peel gets better as it ages. It's also used in Chinese medicine for fevers, coughs, and as an antidote for fish and shellfish poisoning.

SAMBAL—This spicy, multipurpose chili paste or sauce, with countless variations, is primarily made with ripe and red ground or pureed chilies, often with other herbs, spices, and vinegar; shrimp paste or anchovies; and sometimes citrus added. It's popular throughout Southeast Asia and southern India, and you'll find it in Asian food sections of many grocery stores alongside sriracha. (My version of the sauce is on page 152.)

SHAOXING WINE—This amber-colored, shelf-stable rice wine is made with glutinous rice and sometimes additional grains. There are different types and grades, but steer clear of anything labeled "cooking wine." In a pinch, both dry sherry and sake are acceptable cooking substitutes. I usually choose a *nu'er hong* Shaoxing wine for my cooking needs. *Nu'er* means daughter in Chinese, and the wine was traditionally made when a family's daughter was one month old. It was then buried for years and unearthed to drink on her wedding day.

SICHUAN PEPPERCORNS—These deliciously numbing seed-pods are native to the Sichuan province of China. You use the reddish-brown pod husks, not the black seeds, which are gritty when ground and usually removed before packaging. Sichuan peppercorns keep for months in an airtight container. Use them whole and/or grind them at home, since preground Sichuan and Sichuan blends are generally less fresh and pungent and contain unsavory additives. Confusingly, you'll often find Sichuan peppercorns labeled as *sansho* (a related plant) or prickly ash (the family of plants that produce Sichuan peppercorns). Sichuan peppercorns and prickly ash are largely interchangeable, while Japanese sansho is greenish and has a more citrusy flavor.

DUMPLING FUN FOR KIDS

Including kids in the kitchen from an early age helps them learn the beauty, art, and importance of cooking and eating good food. People often shy away from letting children help because they think kids will either hurt themselves or make a mess. One or both may happen, but you have to start somewhere. I remember being so surprised in college about how many students showed up with no clue how to cook for themselves. We can do better.

Dumplings are excellent to make with kids because they are tactile and sculptural, and if they get messed up, you can just scrap the skin, keep the filling, and start over. All that's lost is a little time, flour, and water. It's fun for children to express themselves through dumplings—tiny works of art that they then get to eat. And there are loads of tiny tools that kids can muck around with too (that I also *love*): tiny tongs, tiny whisks, tiny spatulas, tiny rolling pins, tiny bamboo steamers, et cetera.

Kids can brightly color and boldly flavor their dumpling doughs (see page 52), make all sorts of cool patterned or marbled skins (see page 56), and fill them with surprises like a tiny cube of cheese or a quail egg (see page 153). Think of Play-Doh fun, only they get to eat their creations when they're done! If I could recommend only one dumpling type to try, it would be one of the three XLB dumplings (pages 96–100). Magic.

For best results, don't micromanage kids in the kitchen. Set them up at a table or give them a step stool, provide skins and filling (or guidance for making both) and some simple instructions, and then let them get to work. On their *own*. They'll come to you if they have questions. It's a lesson in trust, as well as in tenderness, creativity, and gentle handiwork. We generally appreciate things that we've made ourselves more than those that are made for us. We understand them better. Dumplings are no different. Sensitive children often shine when it comes to the dumpling way.

DUMPLINGS 101

HOW TO FORM DUMPLINGS

There are so many different ways to shape dumplings. I've included steps for three basic shapes here—shumai, XLB, and pleated crescent—but I highly recommend playing around with other styles as well. The library is your friend: there are heaps of 1960s to '80s cookbooks, particularly Asian ones, with all sorts of creative dumpling shapes. And the processes are often illustrated! Two historic dumpling shapes that I'm particularly fond of are the Phoenix Eye and the Four Seasons. Also, *yunu pei cailang* (Beautiful Lady Marries Gifted Scholar dumplings)—they are wild.

When I started making dumplings twenty-plus years ago, I didn't use any advanced forming techniques. I basically just cinched them up at the top in a loose, organic crescent, and they were beautiful. People stress about forming their dumplings perfectly, but I really hope that you don't. Give these three shapes a whirl, and if none feel right (or even if they do), create your own. It's your dumpling; do what you want! I've included a recommended shape for each recipe—my favorite—but feel free to make whatever shape you want. Remember to enjoy yourself.

I recommend newbie dumpling makers cut or use larger four-inch skins because they are more forgiving when it comes to forming. Remember to always place formed dumplings on a lightly floured surface so they don't stick and lose their bums, and cover them with a dry towel so they don't dry out.

Shumai

This open-top dumpling shape, also a particular type of Chinese dumpling (see page 75), is easy for beginners and often my go-to. It's fun to adorn the open tops with pinches of colorful, crunchy, or spicy garnishes before or after cooking. I also really like to make two-sided dumpling skins for shumai with contrasting color doughs on the inside and outside. If you don't use homemade skins, trim store-bought wonton wrappers into circles or use thin gyoza skins. Thicker gyoza skins are more suitable for pan-frying or boiling.

1 If using store-bought skins, moisten the perimeter of several at once, before filling, by dipping your index finger in water, two to three times per skin, and tracing it along the inside half– to one-inch perimeter of the dumpling skin. This makes it easier to form the tops of the dumplings without any cracking. If you use homemade skins, skip this step, since they should be plenty moist and pliable.

2 Lay a dumpling skin in your nondominant hand, over the upper part of your palm and your fingers, and use a butter knife, flat bamboo spreader, or shallow spoon to place a scant to heaping tablespoon of filling in the center of the skin. Gather the skin up around the filling so that it naturally pleats (expert dumpling formers will purposely fold and articulate each pleat).

3 With one hand, cinch the open top of the dumpling by making a circle with your thumb and index finger, while forming the dumpling and pressing the bottom of it with the palm or fingers of your other hand. This creates a fairly flat base so that the dumpling sits up in the steamer.

4 Garnish the top of the filling before or after steaming, if desired.

XLB

XLB is short for Chinese xiao long bao. In America, this type of dumpling is often referred to as a soup dumpling because of its brothy interior. Soup dumplings have become very popular in the US in the past several years. I always thought that they'd be complicated to make, but it turns out they're easy! Just like with shumai, you can use this fun-to-twist XLB dumpling shape for any of the book's dumpling fillings. Please only use homemade dough for this shape since it requires so much twisting at the top.

1 Start with a thicker ⅛-inch-thick skin; ¹⁄₁₆ inch is trickier to form, cook, and freeze. If you are rolling out skins individually, then make the inner part a bit thicker than the perimeter. If you want to use the XLB shape for a non-soup dumpling, roll it out to the thinner ¹⁄₁₆ inch if you'd prefer, since it won't contain broth.

2 Lay a dumpling skin in your nondominant hand, over the upper part of your palm and your fingers, and use a flat bamboo spreader, butter knife, or shallow spoon to place a scant to heaping tablespoon of filling in the middle.

3 Gather up the dumpling skin and lightly pinch it together at the top. Twist it counterclockwise or clockwise a few times while holding the base to create natural, swirling pleats. I like to enhance the swirl. If there is too much dough on the top—which can be chewy and tough when cooked—simply snip it off with scissors.

Pleated Crescent

Most people think of dumplings in this pleated-on-one-side half-moon form. It's one of the most ubiquitous shapes worldwide. For years, I hand-formed dumplings into crescents without proper pleats. I had an organic approach that was at once easy to shape and beautiful. For this book, I've learned to make all sorts of dumpling forms, and this pleated crescent is now one of my favorites. I enjoy forming the pleats with one hand, while gathering them with the other, and I often don't even have to look while doing it anymore. It doesn't take long to get the hang of. I believe in you.

NOTE: Store-bought skins are generally more rigid, so they accommodate fewer pleats than homemade dough—usually 4 to 5 for store-bought, 6 to 8 for homemade. You can skip pleating altogether and simply seal the top by pinching it or lightly crimping with the tines of a fork.

You can also seal the dumpling first and then pleat it so that both sides of the dumpling are pleated at the top, forming small s's along the seam. Sometimes this is easier with store-bought dough and/or for a beginning dumpling maker.

1 If using store-bought skins, moisten the perimeter of several at once, before filling, by dipping your index finger in water, two to three times per skin, and tracing it along the inside ½- to 1-inch perimeter of the dumpling skin. This makes it easier to form the tops of the dumplings without any cracking. If you use homemade skins, skip this step, since they should be plenty moist and pliable.

2 Lay a dumpling skin in your nondominant hand, over the upper part of your palm and your fingers, and use a butter knife, flat bamboo spreader, or shallow spoon to place a scant to heaping tablespoon of filling in the middle, evening it out a bit while leaving about ½ inch of dumpling skin around the perimeter.

3 Slightly fold up the skin while cupping the dumpling. Starting on one end of the dumpling, pinch and seal the two sides of the skin between your thumb and index finger at around one to two o'clock (if you are right-handed) or ten to eleven o'clock (left-handed). Then make your first pleat by pinching and pressing the pleat with your nondominant hand toward your dominant hand, which gathers. Continue making several more pleats on one side using one hand to form pleats and the other to gather.

4 Once the dumpling is formed, place it on a lightly floured work surface, piece of parchment or waxed paper, or silicone mat to slightly flatten the bottom, and then reinforce the pleats by pinching them from one side of the dumpling to the other. If the wings at either end of the pleated dumpling stick out too much, simply fold them in.

HOW TO COOK DUMPLINGS

At the start of each dumpling recipe, I've included my favored way to cook them, but please use those recommendations, including garnishes, sauces, and dough types, as potential jumping-off points. You can cook most dumplings any of these three ways.

Steaming

Steaming is a culinary art form and an elegant and traditional way to cook dumplings. In fact, it's my favorite way. I love the many different woven bamboo steamer basket shapes and sizes, the under-cover cook time (don't open the lid; the steam will escape!), the dramatic reveal when you finally lift off the lid (I like to do this at the table), and the way the steam wafts up into the room. Moist heat is ideal for delicate dumplings.

1 Fill a steaming pot one-quarter to half full with water, allowing 3 to 5 inches between the water and the steamer, and bring to a boil over high heat.

2 Lightly oil the steamer, or place perforated parchment paper, cheesecloth, or thin cabbage leaves in it. Situate the dumplings inside, leaving ½ to 1 inch between each dumpling. If you are steaming XLB, set the dumplings in lightly oiled Asian soup spoons or tartlet molds. I recommend steaming no more than three stacked tiers at once.

3 Once the water is boiling, carefully place the steamer on the pot, and steam the dumplings for 7 to 10 minutes. As a general rule, shumai-shaped dumplings take 7 to 8 minutes, crescent and XLB 8 to 10.

4 With oven mitts or a kitchen towel, carefully remove the steamer from the pot, and serve the dumplings directly from the steamer or transfer them with tongs to a platter. If serving directly from the steamer, set it on a plate or platter to capture drippings if you like. Remove the lid at the table for grand, steamy effect!

STEAMING FROZEN DUMPLINGS: Add 2 to 3 minutes to the steam time.

STEAMING GLUTEN-FREE RICE FLOUR DUMPLINGS: Steam these dumplings for only 5 to 6 minutes since they become waterlogged and overly sticky if you cook them too long.

ROTATING THE STEAMER: It's not a bad idea to rotate the steamer halfway through steaming, but it's not imperative. If you are steaming vegetables or other foods in the steamer also, or have different-sized and -shaped dumplings, then I recommend you do rotate since both can lead to uneven cooking.

STEAMING OTHER FOODS: When steaming vegetables (or shellfish, or other yumminess) with your dumplings, either in the same tray or another, use smaller and more tender vegetables or foods with similar cook times. You can also chop them to size, blanch them first, or start steaming them ahead of time so that everything is fully cooked and ready at the same time. Always place dumplings in the basket closest to the water so that they steam evenly and fully.

Pan-Frying

Pan-fried dumplings, a.k.a. potstickers, are often the gateway dumpling for home cooks. They're fast, easy, and yummy, and all you need to make them is a pan with a lid and a little oil. I love pan-fried dumplings. You get the best of both dumpling worlds—fried on the bottom, steamed on the top. I also really enjoy the dramatic way you add water to the pan once the dumplings are partly cooked, which loudly crackles and pops, before smashing down the lid to contain all the hot and steamy goodness.

1 In a large nonstick skillet over medium heat, preheat 1 to 2 tablespoons vegetable oil (peanut adds great flavor; I usually use canola). Once hot, after about 1 minute, add the dumplings to the pan with the pleated/pinched side up, with ½ to 1 inch between each. I like to place them in a circle with some in the middle. A large pan should fit fifteen to twenty.

2 Fry the dumplings for 2 to 3 minutes, until the bottoms are golden. Quickly add ⅓ cup water to the pan (you could also use flavorful broth), being careful not to burn yourself, and immediately cover it with a lid. The oil and water will loudly and dramatically splatter.

3 Reduce the heat to medium low and cook for 5 to 6 minutes, until the water is mostly absorbed and the pan is quiet. Halfway through, check the bottom of a dumpling by carefully picking it up with tongs or chopsticks. You want a nice golden brown. Reduce the heat if it is too dark, and raise it if not dark enough. Quickly nudge all the dumplings around so that they don't stick to the pan. Cover again.

4 Once the dumplings have absorbed most of the water, remove the lid, slightly reduce the heat, and cook for 1 to 2 more minutes, until they have a medium-brown crust on the bottom.

5 Transfer the dumplings to a paper towel–lined plate. Serve them bottom side up so they stay nice and crispy.

PAN-FRYING FROZEN DUMPLINGS: Add 2 to 3 minutes to step 3 (7 to 9 minutes total). Also, add 1 to 2 more tablespoons of water—so, ⅓ cup plus 1 to 2 tablespoons—to compensate for the slightly drier frozen skin.

PAN-FRYING GLUTEN-FREE RICE FLOUR DUMPLINGS: Add slightly more water to the pan when pan-frying these dumplings and cook for slightly less time. Start with ⅓ cup plus 2 tablespoons (rice flour is thirsty!). Fry for 2 to 3 minutes at the beginning, only 3 to 4 minutes once covered, and 1 to 2 minutes with the lid off.

POTSTICKER LACE: I've tried my hand at potsticker lace and ultimately don't dig it. It's a fairly new technique that seems Instagram fueled (it's photogenic), where you add a slurry of flour or cornstarch plus water to your dumpling pan to create a fried, lacy base that connects the dumplings. It looks fine, but I don't like eating the greasy flour bits. If you do decide to try this, I recommend using rice flour plus water. I had the best crisping results with it.

Boiling

Boiling is a simple and beautiful way to cook dumplings, and boiled dumplings are particularly comforting when the weather is cold or you or a loved one are under the weather. So is dumpling soup. If you aren't boiling them in broth, be sure to salt the cooking water as you would for pasta. It helps to season the skins and seal the dough, preventing waterlogged dumplings.

Always properly form and reinforce dumplings before boiling so you don't end up with an exploded dumpling stew. It's best to boil crescents, but XLB dumplings work as well. Obviously, don't boil open-topped shumai. For crescents, you can fold their ends into each other and press them together for reinforcement, into a tortellini-like shape.

1 Fill a large pot three-quarters full with salted water or broth and bring to a boil over high heat. Add 8 to 10 dumplings to the pot, and gently nudge them around with a spoon for the first minute or so, making sure that they don't stick to the bottom of the pot or each other. Once the water returns to a boil, reduce the heat to medium low to maintain a low boil, just above a simmer.

2 Cook for a total of 5 to 6 minutes, until the skins are slightly translucent and puffy, and the dumplings have been floating for at least 2 to 3 minutes.

3 Gently remove the dumplings from the pot with a large slotted spoon, spider (or skimmer), or handled sieve, and serve immediately.

NOTE: Store-bought dumpling skins are generally thinner than homemade and typically take a minute or so less to boil.

Also, you can reuse the water or broth twice; more than that and the skins will get tacky from residual starch.

BOILING FROZEN DUMPLINGS: Add 2 to 3 minutes to the boil time.

BOILING GLUTEN-FREE RICE FLOUR DUMPLINGS: Boil these dumplings for only 4 to 5 minutes since they become waterlogged and overly sticky if you cook them too long.

COOKING WITH BROTH: The first time I had dumplings cooked in a flavorful and fatty chicken stock, I saw the light. The tasty broth gave the skins so much flavor and left them with a gorgeous sheen. There are so many ways to cook dumplings with broth. You can boil them and drain them, reserving the broth for another use; you can serve the dumplings with a cup or bowl of the broth on the side; or you can make dumpling soup (see page 147).

DUMPLING DOUGHS

Dumpling doughs come in many shapes and sizes, and I've included three primary ones for you here—All-Purpose Egg (page 42), All-Purpose Eggless (page 47), and Gluten-Free Rice Flour (page 49). These are all informed by and in the manner of traditional, straightforward Asian dumpling doughs, but they work well with all sorts of dumplings.

Keep in mind that although I've included a recommended dough for each recipe, most dumplings can be made with any of the book's doughs (any exceptions are noted). Have fun, feel free, and be creative, adding powdered herbs, spices, vegetables, and fruits to your dumpling doughs (see page 52), or combining various doughs if you are making art skins (see page 56).

It's perfectly fine to use store-bought skins for most of the book's dumplings except the XLB. That said, homemade skins are superior. As with pasta dough, fresh dumpling dough is a bit more wet and pliable. One of the best attributes of homemade skins is that they stretch; store-bought skins are usually quite dry and not very flexible.

The downside is that making dumpling dough from scratch takes time. With that in mind, I've included a lot of tips and tricks for streamlining the dough-making process. If you mix your dough with a stand mixer or food processor, as I often do, and roll it out with a pasta roller, you can go from start to finish with these doughs—with fifty to sixty cut skins plus resting time—in less than an hour. And while the dough rests, you can make the filling!

Having helpers on hand to fill and form the dumplings will make quick work of it too.

With all three doughs, I recommend pulling off a quarter of the dough at a time, forming and filling the twelve to fifteen dumplings you make from it, and then setting into cooking or freezing them before rolling out and cutting the next quarter. Work in batches so the skins and dumplings don't stick to any surfaces or dry out. If you're having a dumpling-making party (see page 162) or working with others, then by all means, go ahead and do it all at once in an assembly line.

REFRIGERATING AND FREEZING DOUGHS

I often make dumpling doughs ahead of time to spread out tasks. You can refrigerate any of the doughs that follow—the all-purpose doughs for two to three days; the rice flour dough for up to one—and freeze both all-purpose doughs for up to one month (don't freeze the rice dough). Always wrap the dough tightly in plastic wrap, and put it in an additional plastic bag when freezing. Don't forget to label and date the bag! (I don't recommend freezing or refrigerating rolled skins because they so easily stick to one another even when well dusted with flour or cornstarch.)

When you're ready to use refrigerated dough, remove it from the refrigerator two to three hours in advance, unwrap it, then cover it with a damp towel and an inverted bowl. If you are in a rush, warm the dough by intermittently enclosing it with your hands and pressing it to speed things along. For frozen dough, either put it fully wrapped in the refrigerator overnight (twelve to fifteen hours) to thaw before proceeding with the damp towel and bowl, or remove it from the freezer four to five hours in advance, unwrapping and covering it as noted.

ROLLING OUT DOUGHS

Ideal Thickness and Diameter

This is, of course, somewhat up to personal preference, but I generally recommend rolling doughs out to about one-sixteenth inch for shumai and crescent dumplings and to a thicker one-eighth inch for XLB. If you are rolling out dough using a Marcato Atlas pasta machine or a KitchenAid pasta-roller attachment, the former is often #5 and the latter is often #4. Thicker dough is always easier to work with because it is more forgiving and easier to form, so start thicker and move toward thin.

When it's time to cut, for ease of filling, forming, and cooking, larger is better—I recommend starting with four-inch-diameter skins. In general, smaller skins are harder to hold and shape, but I do think they are worth striving for. I prefer my dumplings as close to one or two bites as possible.

Note that dough sheets will naturally cinch up a bit after rolling and cutting, so a four-inch-diameter, one-sixteenth-inch-thick skin becomes more like three and three-quarter inches in diameter and one-twelfth inch thick when you fill it.

Dusting with Flour

Use whatever flour is called for in the dough recipe to lightly dust skins and formed dumplings to prevent sticking. I intentionally call for easy-to-source all-purpose, rice, and tapioca flours for the primary doughs in this book, but feel free to experiment with others. I recommend starting with low-protein, finely milled flours for dumpling dough.

I also like to use grittier semolina flour for dusting, common in pasta making, because I like the feel of it and it is less sticky when it comes into contact with water. Use it sparingly though. If you're boiling dumplings, fantastic—the semolina will boil off; however, be sure not to use much if steaming or pan-frying.

Note that you'll want to avoid stacking dumpling skins if possible. If you must stack them for space reasons, never stack more than ten at a time.

AVOIDING COMMON PITFALLS

When dough is overworked, or sometimes when it's too wet, dry, or cold, it can become craggy and fall apart. If you're using a pasta roller, the dough will often slow down the machine and get stuck. If this happens, pat both sides of the dough with flour and press your fingertips into it, massaging both sides a bit before passing it through the machine again. Sometimes you'll need to fold and refold before hand- or machine-rolling the well-dusted sheet (a.k.a. laminating) as well; this will usually do the trick. If it cannot be salvaged, toss it and start over.

Another potential issue is when dumpling dough gets floppy or tacky. This can happen depending on the flour type, contact with your hands or roller, and the temperature or humidity of your kitchen. If this happens, add more flour incrementally while kneading and laminating. Both will add strength, elasticity, and smoothness to the dough.

ALL-PURPOSE EGG DOUGH *Vegetarian*

If I had to use one dumpling dough for the rest of my life, this would be it. I value the straightforward simplicity of it. The eggs add protein, bite, and strength, and it works well and tastes yummy with added herbs, spices, and powdered veggies and fruits (see page 52). If you are just getting started in the wide world of dumpling making, try this dough first since it's easiest to work with.

MAKES ABOUT 1½ POUNDS OF DOUGH FOR 50 TO 60 (3- TO 4-INCH) DUMPLING SKINS

- 2 large eggs
- ½ cup plus 2 tablespoons hot water (110 to 120 degrees F)
- 1 teaspoon vegetable oil
- ½ teaspoon kosher salt
- 3 to 3¼ cups (425 to 475 grams) all-purpose flour, plus more for dusting

CHOOSE YOUR OWN KNEADING AND FORMING ADVENTURE

FIRST . . .

MIXING AND KNEADING BY HAND

1 In a medium bowl, whisk the eggs, water, oil, and salt for 1 to 2 minutes, until the eggs become slightly frothy.

2 In another medium bowl, whisk 3 cups of the flour to break up any clumps. Make a small well in the center of the flour, and slowly blend in the egg mixture. I like to use chopsticks for this; a wooden spoon works too. Mix the dough together until it forms a shaggy mass.

3 Knead the dough for about 3 minutes in the bowl. Put the shaggy bits from around the bottom and edges of the bowl into the middle of the dough, and close it around them. If the dough seems stiff, wet your hands with water and knead

it until it becomes more elastic. If it is too wet and sticking to your hands, add flour 1 tablespoon at a time, working it into the dough.

4 Lightly dust your work surface with flour, turn out the dough, and knead it for 4 to 5 more minutes, until it is smooth and elastic. Again, if the dough seems stiff, wet your hands with water and knead it until it becomes more elastic. If it is too wet and sticking, add flour to your work surface 1 tablespoon at a time, and knead it into the dough.

5 Cover the dough with a slightly damp towel, and put it under the inverted mixing bowl. Rest it for 30 minutes (or up to 2 hours) before rolling it out for dumplings, or refrigerating or freezing it (see page 3).

OR

. . . WITH A STAND MIXER

1 In the bowl of a stand mixer fitted with the hook attachment, mix 3 cups of the flour on medium-low speed (#2 on a KitchenAid) for about 30 seconds.

2 In a medium bowl, whisk the eggs, water, salt, and oil for 1 to 2 minutes, until the eggs become slightly frothy. With the mixer on medium-low speed, add the egg mixture to the flour in a slow, steady stream; this should take 40 to 50 seconds. Once fully incorporated, stop the machine and pinch the dough. It should hold its shape and not stick to your fingers. If the dough is too wet or too dry, add water or flour by teaspoon or tablespoon, respectively.

3 Lock the mixer head and mix on medium speed (#4 on a KitchenAid) for 30 seconds to 1 minute, until the dough forms a ball beside or around the hook.

4 Lightly dust your work surface with flour, turn out the dough, and put any left-behind shaggy bits into the middle of the dough. Knead it for 1 to 2 minutes, until it is smooth and elastic.

5 Cover the dough with a slightly damp towel, and put it under the inverted mixing bowl. Rest it for 30 minutes (or up to 2 hours) before rolling it out for dumplings, or refrigerating or freezing it (see page 3).

THEN . . . ▶

MAKING ALL-PURPOSE DOUGHS IN A FOOD PROCESSOR

Both all-purpose doughs (Egg or Eggless) can quickly and easily be made with a food processor. For either, put the flour in the bowl of the food processor and pulse 4 to 5 times. Then add the wet ingredients (whisked eggs, water, oil, and salt for Egg; water, oil, and salt for Eggless) in a slow, steady stream for 40 to 50 seconds. Continue processing for 20 to 30 seconds, until the dough forms a ball. Remove the lid and pinch the dough. It should hold its shape and not stick to your fingers. If it is too wet or too dry, add flour or water by teaspoon or tablespoon, respectively. Process for another 10 to 15 seconds, then proceed with steps 4 and 5 of Mixing and Kneading by Hand (see page 43), kneading for 2 to 3 minutes rather than 4 to 5.

FORMING SKINS BY HAND

6 Use your thumbs to poke a hole in the center of the dough. Gradually enlarge the hole with both hands, by moving the dough clockwise or counterclockwise, until it is about ¾ to 1 inch in diameter.

7 Using a bench scraper, if you have one, or a sharp knife, slice the dough into 10 to 15 (¾- to 1-inch) pieces at a time. Roll each piece into a ball and then place it on the lightly floured work surface, making sure none are touching. Cover the balls and the remaining dough with a dry towel.

8 Lightly flour the work surface again, smash a ball with your palm or a flat, heavy object (a tortilla press works), and then roll it into a 3- to 4-inch–diameter skin (about 1⁄16 inch thick for shumai or crescents, and ⅛ inch thick for XLB). Don't worry if it isn't perfectly round.

9 Dust the skins with flour as you make them, and place them with minimal overlap on your lightly floured surface, covered with a dry towel. Try not to stack them, to eliminate sticking—space permitting, of course. Always keep the balled dough covered with a dry towel too so that it doesn't dry out.

NOTE: Prepare the skins quickly and expertly, like a pro, by using your primary hand to roll them with a small dowel rolling pin (see page 10) while, in between rolls, twisting the skin in ½- to 1-inch increments clockwise or counterclockwise with your other hand. Flip the skin about halfway through.

... WITH A COOKIE CUTTER

6 Lightly dust your work surface with flour. Divide the dough into 4 equal pieces. Take 1 piece, covering the other 3 with a dry towel, and shape it by hand into a rounded rectangle about ½ inch thick. Using a rolling pin, roll it out until it is about $\frac{1}{16}$ inch thick (or ⅛ inch thick if making XLB). Sprinkle the dough and your rolling pin with flour if the dough gets sticky.

7 Using a 3- to 4-inch cookie cutter, cut out as many skins as you can, usually 10 to 12 per piece if $\frac{1}{16}$ inch thick, and 6 to 8 if ⅛ inch thick. Collect the leftover dough, and reform and reroll it as described. I recommend rerolling two to three times, until the dough is no longer pliable.

OR

... WITH A PASTA ROLLER

6 Lightly dust your work surface with flour. Divide the dough into 4 equal pieces. Take 1 piece, covering the other 3 with a dry towel, and shape it by hand into a rounded rectangle about ½ inch thick and no wider than your pasta roller. Dust it with flour.

7 Set a hand-crank pasta machine to the widest setting (usually #1), and feed the dough through the roller. If you are using a stand-mixer attachment, set the roller to the widest setting of #1, and with the mixer on medium-low speed (#2 on a KitchenAid), feed the dough through the roller. Move up to the next thinner setting (most machines range from #1 to #6, #7, #8, or #9), and roll it through again. Do this, flouring the dough as necessary before rolling, until you have rolled it through the indicated settings, it is almost translucent, and it is about $\frac{1}{16}$ inch thick for crescents and shumai, or ⅛ inch for XLB.

8 Lay the sheet on the lightly floured work surface, and cut the sheets as detailed in step 7 of Forming Skins with a Cookie Cutter (above). (I recommend rolling, cutting, and filling in 4 separate batches so the dumpling dough does not dry out as it waits to be filled.) Once you've filled the dumplings, either cook, refrigerate, or freeze them.

9 Each sheet should give you about 10 to 12 (3- to 4-inch) skins in the first cutting if $\frac{1}{16}$ inch thick, or 6 to 8 skins if ⅛ inch thick.

10 Collect the leftover dough, and reform and reroll it as described. I recommend rerolling two to three times, until the dough is no longer pliable.

NOTE: If the dough sheet gets large and unwieldy, set it on your lightly floured work surface, cut it in half, and proceed with 2 pieces, one at a time, through the roller.

ALL-PURPOSE EGGLESS DOUGH *Vegan*

This is a beautifully simple dumpling dough, with a light and supple bite, that I've made more times than I can count. I love that you can walk into just about any kitchen in the world and whip these up. Like Devo, you can whip it, into shape! And, like all the doughs in this book, it works great with added herbs, spices, and powdered veggies and fruits (see page 52).

MAKES ABOUT 1½ POUNDS OF DOUGH FOR 50 TO 60 (3- TO 4-INCH) DUMPLING SKINS

× 3 to 3¼ cups (425 to 475 grams) all-purpose flour, plus more for dusting

× ½ teaspoon kosher salt

× 1 cup warm water (90 to 100 degrees F)

× 2 teaspoons vegetable oil

CHOOSE YOUR OWN KNEADING AND FORMING ADVENTURE

MIXING AND KNEADING BY HAND

1 In a medium bowl, whisk 3 cups of the flour to break up any clumps. In a separate bowl, add the salt to the water, and stir to dissolve the salt.

2 Make a small well in the center of the flour, and slowly add the water and then oil to it, while blending them into the flour. I like to use chopsticks for this; a wooden spoon works too. Mix the dough together until it forms a shaggy mass.

3 Knead the dough for about 3 minutes in the bowl. Put the shaggy bits from around the bottom and edges of the bowl into the middle of the dough, and close it around them. If the dough seems stiff, wet your hands with water and knead it until it becomes more elastic. If it is too wet and sticking to your hands, add flour 1 tablespoon at a time, working it into the dough.

4 Lightly dust your work surface with flour, turn out the dough, and knead it for 4 to 5 minutes, until it is smooth and elastic. Again, if the dough seems stiff, wet your hands with water and knead it until it becomes more elastic. If it is too wet and sticking, add flour to your work surface 1 tablespoon at a time, and knead it into the dough.

5 Cover the dough with a slightly damp towel, and put it under the inverted mixing bowl. Rest it for 30 minutes (or up to 2 hours) before rolling it out for dumplings, or refrigerating or freezing it (see page 3).

OR

. . . WITH A STAND MIXER

1 In the bowl of a stand mixer fitted with the hook attachment, mix 3 cups of the flour on medium-low speed (#2 on a KitchenAid) for about 30 seconds.

2 In a separate bowl, add the salt to the water, and stir to dissolve the salt. With the mixer on medium-low speed, add the water and then oil in a slow, steady stream; this should take 40 to 50 seconds. Once they are fully incorporated, stop the machine and pinch the dough. It should hold its shape and not stick to your fingers. If the dough is too wet or too dry, add flour or water by teaspoon or tablespoon, respectively.

3 Lock the mixer head and mix on medium speed (#4 on a KitchenAid) for 30 seconds to 1 minute, until the dough forms a ball beside or around the hook.

4 Lightly dust your work surface with flour, turn out the dough, and put any left-behind shaggy bits into the middle of the dough. Knead it for 1 to 2 minutes, until it is smooth and elastic.

5 Cover the dough with a slightly damp towel, and place it under the inverted mixing bowl. Rest it for 30 minutes (or up to 2 hours) before rolling it out for dumplings, or refrigerating or freezing it (see page 3).

THEN . . .

FORMING SKINS

6 Form the skins according to one of the methods detailed on pages 44–46.

GLUTEN-FREE RICE FLOUR DOUGH *Vegan*

This gorgeous and delicious rice-and-tapioca dough steams, boils, and fries well in slightly less time than the all-purpose doughs. I think it's best shaped as shumai or an unpleated crescent and pan-fried. Keep in mind that this dough must be hand-worked because without gluten it lacks the flexibility and stretch needed to be machine-formed or -rolled. It works well with all the herbs, spices, and powdered veggie and fruit additions, and you can even make art skins with it (see page 56).

MAKES ABOUT 1 POUND OF DOUGH FOR 50 TO 60 (3- TO 3½-INCH) DUMPLING SKINS

- × 1½ cups (180 to 225 grams; see note) glutinous rice flour, plus more for dusting
- × ¾ cup (85 grams) tapioca flour
- × ¼ teaspoon kosher salt
- × ¾ cup plus 3 tablespoons warm water (90 to 100 degrees F)
- × 1 tablespoon vegetable oil, plus more for forming skins

CONTINUED →

MIXING AND KNEADING BY HAND

1 In a medium bowl, whisk the flours. In a separate bowl, add the salt and water, and stir to dissolve the salt.

2 Make a small well in the center of the flour, and slowly add the water and then oil while mixing. I like to use chopsticks for this; a wooden spoon works too. Mix and gather the clumpy pieces until the water and oil has been absorbed by the flour and you can shape the dough into a mass.

3 Knead the dough for about 1 minute in the bowl, until smooth. It's more like squeezing than kneading because it's quite crumbly at first. You want it to gather together, have some give, and not stick to your hands. If the dough is too wet or dry, add glutinous rice flour or water, respectively, 1 teaspoon at a time.

4 Cover the dough with a slightly damp towel and the inverted mixing bowl. Rest it for 8 to 10 minutes before hand-forming it for dumplings or refrigerating it (see page 3). Do not let the dough rest longer than 8 to 10 minutes or it will sag and dry out. Do not freeze the dough.

THEN . . .

NOTE: I highly recommend using Koda Farms Mochiko sweet rice flour for this dough. It is readily available and is my favorite because of its workability and overall quality. Koda Farms is a Japanese American family–owned, California-based farm that has been growing and milling delicious short-grain sweet rice since the 1940s. Rice flours are incredibly diverse in terms of starch composition, workability, and weight. If you use Mochiko, 1½ cups of flour will be 225 grams. Most other brands will be around 180 to 200 grams for the same volume.

FORMING SKINS BY HAND

5 Fill a small bowl with a few tablespoons of oil. Lightly dust a work surface with rice flour. Divide the dough into 4 equal pieces. Take 1 piece, covering the other 3 with a slightly damp towel. Form it into a 1-inch-wide sausage shape, and then cut it into 12 to 15 pieces. Keep them under the slightly damp towel.

6 Remove 1 of the small pieces, put a generous dab of oil on your palm, and roll it into a ball. Gently press down on it with your other hand until it's about 2 inches in diameter. Carefully pull it off your palm and flip it. Continue to press down until it is about 3 inches in diameter, soft and smooth, and about ⅛ inch thick.

7 With the skin still on your palm, use a butter knife, flat bamboo spreader, or shallow spoon to place 1½ to 2 teaspoons of filling in the middle.

8 Gently pull up the sides of the skin and shape the dumpling as either shumai (page 22) or an unpleated crescent (page 26). This dough is *very* easy to tear and break. If you can't work a tear back together with the warmth of your hands and oil, take a small portion of dough from another piece, flatten it, and patch the tear. Once the dumpling is formed, place it on a lightly floured work surface, piece of parchment or waxed paper, or silicone mat to slightly flatten the bottom. Always keep formed dumplings covered with a slightly damp towel.

NOTE: Store this dough on a plate (up to 1 day only) when refrigerating it because it tends to sweat and dry out. The dough freezes well only in dumpling form, not by itself as a ball.

NEXT-LEVEL DOUGHS

COLORFUL FLAVORED DOUGHS

There is a world of beauty and flavor that you can almost effortlessly add to any dumpling dough by using ground herbs and spices and powdered vegetables and fruits. I love to serve up a rainbow of colored dumplings!

I recommend using only powdered and ground ingredients in doughs—the wet, softened particulates in juices, broths, and purees tend to result in gummy, sticky cooked dumpling skins, with a bite much like fruit leather. Despite what you may find online, please trust me on this. I've done a *lot* of testing.

In a blind tasting of these flavored doughs, you would likely be able to identify the herbs and spices; the vegetable and fruit powders, however, vary in intensity. I can always taste nettles and beets in the doughs, but the other flavors can be quite subtle.

DIY versus Store-Bought Powders

If you do decide to use powdered fruits or vegetables in your doughs, you can either dehydrate and grind them yourself (I do this with nettles) or purchase them. Some markets carry them as supplements for smoothies and juices in the health section, and you can also find them online.

I've had a lot of success with Suncore Foods Supercolor Powders (SuncoreFoods.com). I've used the activated charcoal coconut, orange carrot, red beet, pink pitaya/dragon fruit, and blue butterfly pea powders. Most are organic, and all contain no additives and are packaged in small resealable bags. You can make several batches of dumpling dough with each bag.

Recommendations and Uses

I list recommendations for various flavor and color options here, but I especially like to mix and match different colored doughs for art skins (see page 56). Some favorites include carrot plus charcoal "zebra" skins; marbled blue butterfly pea and bright pink pitaya/dragon fruit with green matcha skins; and turmeric or curry skins studded with toasted black sesame or poppy seeds.

Have fun and be creative! Increase or decrease the amount of each powder and spice depending on how flavorful and colorful you want the skins to be. You also might need to add a tablespoon or more of water to a dough when incorporating these ingredients—feel it out.

When using powders, herbs, or spices, whisk them with the flour to eliminate any clumps; if the ingredient is particularly clumpy, break it up first. For the Gluten-Free Rice Flour Dough (page 49), you should roughly halve all recommended amounts.

ADDITION	AMOUNT	DUMPLINGS	NOTES
Beet powder	3 to 4 tablespoons for all-purpose doughs; 1½ to 2 tablespoons for gluten-free rice flour dough	Beet & Turmeric Rice (page 84), Orange Chicken (page 73)	
Butterfly pea powder	3 to 4 tablespoons for all-purpose doughs; 1½ to 2 tablespoons for gluten-free rice flour dough	Mapo Tofu (page 102), any XLB (pages 96–100)	
Carrot powder	3 to 4 tablespoons for all-purpose doughs; 1½ to 2 tablespoons for gluten-free rice flour dough	Beef Curry (page 81), Chawan Mushi Egg (page 79), Orange Chicken (page 73), Shrimp & Grits (page 125)	
Charcoal powder	1 to 2 tablespoons for all-purpose doughs; ½ to 1 tablespoon for gluten-free rice flour dough	Beet & Turmeric Rice (page 84), Coconut-Sesame (page 89)	*Be careful because charcoal can be quite messy when loose*
Cocoa powder	3 to 4 tablespoons for all-purpose doughs; 1½ to 2 tablespoons for gluten-free rice flour dough	Bananas Foster (page 129), Coconut-Sesame (page 89)	*Plus 1 tablespoon confectioners' sugar for all-purpose doughs; ½ tablespoon for gluten-free rice flour dough*
Curry powder	2 teaspoons for all-purpose doughs; 1 teaspoon for gluten-free rice flour dough	Beef Curry (page 81), Gingery Cabbage & Mushroom (page 60)	
Dragon fruit powder	3 to 4 tablespoons for all-purpose doughs; 1½ to 2 tablespoons for gluten-free rice flour dough	Beet & Turmeric Rice (page 84), any XLB (pages 96–100)	
Five-spice powder	2 teaspoons for all-purpose doughs; 1 teaspoon for gluten-free rice flour dough	Cincinnati Chili (page 118), Mapo Tofu (page 102), any XLB (pages 96–100)	

ADDITION	AMOUNT	DUMPLINGS	NOTES
Matcha	1 to 2 tablespoons for all-purpose doughs; ½ to 1 tablespoon for gluten-free rice flour dough	Chawan Mushi Egg (page 79), Salmon-Sesame (page 63), any XLB (pages 96–100)	
Nettle powder	3 to 4 tablespoons for all-purpose doughs; 1½ to 2 tablespoons for gluten-free rice flour dough	Morel–Sherry Cream (page 108), Nettle & Caramelized Onion (page 113)	
Poppy seeds	2 to 4 tablespoons for all-purpose doughs; 1 to 2 tablespoons for gluten-free rice flour dough	Bananas Foster (page 129), Salmon-Sesame (page 63)	*Seeds work best with ⅛-inch-thick skins; if rolled to ¹⁄₁₆ inch, they may tear*
Sesame seeds (white or black), toasted	2 to 4 tablespoons for all-purpose doughs; not recommended for gluten-free rice flour dough	Beet & Turmeric Rice (page 84), Coconut-Sesame (page 89), Salmon-Sesame (page 63)	*Seeds work best with ⅛-inch-thick skins; if rolled to ¹⁄₁₆ inch, they may tear; black seeds are most dramatic*
Smoked paprika	1 to 2 tablespoons for all-purpose doughs, ½ to 1 tablespoon for gluten-free rice flour dough	Morel–Sherry Cream (page 108), Nettle & Caramelized Onion (page 113)	
Spirulina powder	1 to 2 tablespoons for all-purpose doughs; ½ to 1 tablespoon for gluten-free rice flour dough	Beet & Turmeric Rice (page 84), Chawan Mushi Egg (page 79), Orange Chicken (page 73)	
Turmeric (ground)	2 teaspoons for all-purpose doughs; 1 teaspoon for gluten-free rice flour dough	Beef Curry (page 81), Beet & Turmeric Rice (page 84), Gingery Cabbage & Mushroom (page 60), Salmon-Sesame (page 63)	

ART SKINS

There are *so* many fun things that you can do with colorful doughs. In fact, I could write an entire book on the topic! Instead, I've detailed a few techniques on my website at LizCrain.com/DumplingsEqualLove as bonus material. Please use that as a jumping-off point and post your wild creations on social media with the tag *#dumplingsequal love*. Some of my favorite art skins are marbled (twisting together two to three different doughs), dotted, striped and spiraled, and two sided (combining two different colored dough sheets).

Art skins are often my favorite part of dumpling making because you never know exactly how they will turn out until you cook them. In that way, it's similar to dyeing eggs or glazing ceramics—another reason why kids (and young-at-heart adults!) really dig it.

Bench scrapers are a good tool for gently pulling art skins off lightly floured surfaces, fondant punchers are perfect for making cool designs, and manual or mechanized pasta rollers make the whole process less labor intensive. Always remember to fill your dumplings on the least creative and colorful side so that when you cook them, your favored art shows on the outside.

Be aware that while the Gluten-Free Rice Flour Dough (page 49) will work with powdered additions, since it's delicate and needs to be hand-formed, you can't use most of the art-skin techniques successfully with it. My favorite approach with this dough is to form the skins with the plain dough, then push little pea-sized balls of another flavored, colored dough into them before flipping them over to fill them. You get cool little polka dots that way.

ASIAN-ORIGIN DUMPLINGS

When most people think of dumplings, their minds go straight to Asian-origin ones that are popular worldwide, such as Japanese gyoza, Chinese xiao long bao ("soup dumplings"), or Korean mandu—and there are recipes for all of these wonderful dumplings included here.

My love of dumplings began with Chinese shumai and quickly evolved to include a wide array of mostly Chinese, as well as other Asian, dumplings. I learned a lot from others when developing the recipes for this chapter—primarily authors of out-of-print cookbooks (see page 169), and folks in my city. The Japanese gyoza and Korean mandu are family recipes from Portlanders I deeply respect. For many of the recipes, I hit the books with the help of my Multnomah County Library research librarian friend Pauline Theriault. Travel also often played an integral part in inspiration. The process was as enjoyable as the results.

Now it's time to pull out those bamboo steamers, a lazy Susan if you have one, and some small dipping sauce bowls, and get cooking!

GINGERY CABBAGE & MUSHROOM *Vegan*

CHINA

SHAPE: Crescent

COOK: Pan-fry

SKIN: All-Purpose
Eggless Dough
(page 47)

GARNISH: Finely
grated carrot or
thinly sliced scallions

SAUCE: Soy-Lime
(page 154), Gyoza
(page 155), Sambal
(page 152), or Chili
Oil (page 150)

During college one summer, I checked out *Florence Lin's Complete Book of Chinese Noodles, Dumplings and Breads* from the library and copied her vegetarian jiao recipe before driving cross-country to visit one of my best friends, Raquel. Together we cooked the delicious dumplings in her Haight-Ashbury apartment. My other best friend, Beth, was also in San Francisco at the time, so we all enjoyed homemade su jiao together. I'll never forget the empowering realization that armed with a good cookbook, I could make just about anything.

Lin's recipe was the inspiration for these crazy-tasty dumplings. Raquel and I still make them together. And when we do, we always freeze some. The comfort of future dumplings helps ease the sadness of goodbye.

MAKES 4½ TO 5 CUPS OF FILLING FOR 50 TO 60 DUMPLINGS

- × 1½ pounds All-Purpose Eggless Dough, or 60 store-bought dumpling skins
- × 4 to 6 dried whole-cap medium shiitake (black) mushrooms (see note)
- × 4 tablespoons peanut oil, divided
- × 1 pound fresh cremini or white button mushrooms, finely diced (see note)

- × 2 tablespoons soy sauce
- × 2 teaspoons sugar
- × ½ pound green cabbage, finely diced (see note)
- × ½ cup finely diced celery
- × 2 tablespoons minced or finely grated peeled fresh ginger
- × 4 cloves garlic, minced or pressed

- × 4 to 6 scallions (both white and green parts), thinly sliced
- × 1 to 2 serrano chilies, minced
- × 1½ to 2 teaspoons kosher salt
- × 1 tablespoon toasted sesame oil

CONTINUED

1 Prepare the dough according to the instructions on page 47, or set out the store-bought skins.

2 Fill a small pot halfway with water, bring to a boil over high heat, and remove from the heat. Add the dried mushrooms to the pot and fully submerge them under a smaller lid or plate. Let them steep for 40 to 50 minutes, until soft.

3 Using a slotted spoon, remove the mushrooms from the pot, reserving the water, and then using your hands, squeeze out and discard the excess water from them. Trim and finely dice them.

4 Meanwhile, in a large skillet over medium-high heat, preheat 2 tablespoons of the peanut oil. Once hot, after 1 to 2 minutes, add both types of mushrooms to the pan, and cook, stirring occasionally, for 1 to 2 minutes, until they begin to soften.

5 Add the soy sauce, sugar, and ½ cup of the reserved mushroom water (be careful to leave any grit from the mushrooms behind). Cook for 5 to 7 minutes, stirring occasionally, until the mushrooms are dry. Transfer the mushrooms to a baking sheet in an even layer, and set them aside to cool.

6 In the same skillet over medium-high heat, preheat the remaining 2 tablespoons of peanut oil. Once hot, after 1 to 2 minutes, add the cabbage, celery, ginger, garlic, scallions, and chilies. Cook for 5 to 6 minutes, stirring occasionally, until the vegetables are dry.

7 Add the salt to taste and the sesame oil, and return the mushrooms to the pan. Cook for 1 to 2 minutes to incorporate. Transfer the filling to the baking sheet in an even layer, and set it aside to cool to room temperature for about 30 minutes. Once cooled, cover and refrigerate for at least 30 minutes before using.

8 Form the dumplings according to the instructions on pages 44–46.

9 Pan-fry the dumplings according to the instructions on page 31.

NOTE: If you prefer to use fresh shiitakes instead of dried, finely dice about 4 ounces, skip the reconstitution steps, and use ¼ cup water in place of the reserved mushroom liquid.

To save time, you can pulse rough-chopped cabbage and cremini mushrooms separately in a food processor to finely dice them. Just know that the yield will be slightly less if you do so.

SALMON-SESAME

CHINA

SHAPE: Shumai

COOK: Steam

SKIN: Turmeric All-
Purpose Egg Dough
(page 42)

GARNISH: Salmon
roe or flying fish roe
(a.k.a. *tobiko*), or
thinly sliced garlic
chives

SAUCE: Citrusy
Sambal–Sour Cream
(page 160), Sesame-
Lime (page 158), or
Soy-Lime (page 154)

When I landed in Portland in my midtwenties, the Pacific Northwest wooed me straightaway with its salt- and freshwater bounty—its dreamy, minerally oysters; freshest-of-the-fresh Oregon spot prawns; lobster-outshining Dungeness crab; and, of course, salmon. Salmon is as beautiful as it is delicious. I love its anadromous life course and how several of its species have shaped Pacific Northwest culture for thousands of years. These dumplings are simple and citrusy so that the salmon shines bright. The Shaoxing wine, soy sauce, sesame oil, garlic chives, and ginger give it the flavor of some of my favorite Chinese salmon dishes. I highly recommend making your own preserved lemons (see page 111) for these.

MAKES 4½ TO 5 CUPS OF FILLING FOR 50 TO 60 DUMPLINGS

- 1½ pounds Turmeric All-Purpose Egg Dough, or 60 store-bought dumpling skins
- 2 pounds salmon, skinned (see note) and chopped into 2- to 3-inch pieces
- ¼ cup freshly squeezed lemon juice (from about 1 medium lemon)
- 2 tablespoons soy sauce
- 2 tablespoons Shaoxing wine, sake, or dry sherry
- 2 egg whites
- 3 tablespoons peanut oil
- 3 tablespoons toasted sesame oil
- ¾ to 1½ teaspoons kosher salt
- ¼ to ½ teaspoon freshly ground black pepper
- 2 cups thinly sliced garlic chives
- 2 tablespoons finely grated or minced peeled fresh ginger
- 1 tablespoon rinsed, minced preserved lemon (about 1 lemon quarter), pith removed and discarded, or 3 tablespoons finely grated fresh lemon zest

CONTINUED ▷

1 Prepare the dough according to the instructions on page 42, or set out the store-bought skins.

2 In the bowl of a food processor, combine the salmon, lemon juice, soy sauce, and wine, and pulse 10 to 15 times, until the fish is roughly chopped. Use a spatula to scrape the sides of the bowl. (Or mince the salmon by hand into a chunky paste and proceed with a spoon.)

3 Add the egg whites, oils, and salt and pepper to taste, and pulse 15 to 20 times, until it's fairly pureed.

4 Transfer the filling to a large bowl, and fold in the chives, ginger, and preserved lemon until evenly distributed.

5 Cover and refrigerate for at least 30 minutes before using.

6 Form the dumplings according to the instructions on pages 44–46.

7 Steam the dumplings according to the instructions on page 28.

NOTE: Salmon skin is tricky to remove, so sometimes I'll ask the fishmonger to do it for me. They make quick, skillful work of it. I really like salmon skin baked or fried, so I always ask them to include it in my package. You could also substitute tuna or trout here if you prefer.

Instead of garlic chives, you can use 10 to 12 thinly sliced scallions (both white and green parts), plus 2 minced or pressed garlic cloves.

OTHER USES FOR FILLING

I often use tackier dumpling fillings like the Pork & Shrimp Shumai (page 75), Orange Chicken (page 73), and Salmon-Sesame (page 63) to make meatballs and patties for soups, stews, noodles, banh mi, sliders, and more. Form the filling into balls or patties, roll them in panko or flour if you want, and pan-fry, boil, broil, or steam them.

Looser dumpling fillings are yummy in stir-fries or fried rice. And, of course, a lot of the fillings in this book can stand alone, including the Mapo Tofu (page 102, great with sticky rice), Bananas Foster (page 129, serve with vanilla ice cream), Crain Family Chili (page 122, yummy *all* the ways), and Garlic-Cheese Grits Casserole (page 126, eaten straight up).

PORK & KIMCHI MANDU

KOREA

SHAPE: Crescent

COOK: Steam

SKIN: All-Purpose Eggless Dough (page 47)

GARNISH: Minced kimchi, thinly sliced scallions, or toasted sesame seeds

SAUCE: Soy-Lime (page 154), Gyoza (page 155), or red Tabasco plus soy sauce

Mandu is Korean for dumpling, and making and cooking them at home is a delicious, time-honored Korean tradition, especially during Lunar New Year. These juicy, spicy, pork-and-tofu-loaded mandu were very popular at a suburban Portland Korean restaurant owned by my friend Chong Choi (co-owner of Choi's Kimchi Company with her son Matt), which closed several years ago. At Chong's restaurant, many patrons dipped their mandu in soy sauce aided by several strong shakes of traditional red Tabasco. I love how this marries a classic Asian ferment with a quintessential American one.

MAKES 4½ TO 5 CUPS OF FILLING FOR 50 TO 60 DUMPLINGS

- 1½ pounds All-Purpose Eggless Dough, or 60 store-bought dumpling skins
- ¼ pound firm tofu
- 1½ cups napa cabbage kimchi (recipe follows), finely diced
- 2 ounces dried sweet potato noodles or thin vermicelli rice noodles
- ¼ pound mung bean sprouts
- ½ pound ground pork or beef, or a mixture
- 2 large eggs
- 3 to 4 scallions (both white and green parts), thinly sliced
- 2 teaspoons minced or pressed garlic
- 2 teaspoons minced or finely grated peeled fresh ginger
- 1 tablespoon toasted sesame oil
- 2 to 3 tablespoons coarse *gochugaru* (dried Korean red pepper flakes)
- 1 to 2 teaspoons kosher salt
- ½ to 1 teaspoon freshly ground black pepper

CONTINUED

1 Prepare the dough according to the instructions on page 47, or set out the store-bought skins.

2 Wrap the tofu in a paper towel, put it on a plate, and place a heavy plate firmly on top of it. Let the tofu drain for at least 15 minutes. In a large bowl, break up the tofu with your fingers so that it resembles finely crumbled feta cheese.

3 Squeeze the kimchi with your hands to remove any excess moisture, and add it to the bowl.

4 Fill a medium pot three-quarters full with water and bring to a boil over high heat. Add the noodles and boil for 7 to 8 minutes, until chewy with some bite. Drain them in a colander, rinse with cold water until cool, and squeeze with your hands to remove excess moisture. Finely chop the noodles and add them to the bowl.

5 Fill a small pot three-quarters full with water and bring to a boil over high heat. Add the bean sprouts, cover, and reduce the heat to medium. Simmer for 6 to 7 minutes, until the sprouts have wilted. Drain them in the colander, rinse with cold water until cool, and squeeze with your hands to remove excess moisture. Finely chop the sprouts and add them to the bowl.

6 Add the pork, eggs, scallions, garlic, ginger, oil, and gochugaru, salt, and pepper to taste. Stir with a fork to break up the pork and egg yolks, then finish mixing by hand or spoon. Cover and refrigerate for at least 30 minutes before using.

7 Form the dumplings according to the instructions on pages 44–46.

8 Steam the dumplings according to the instructions on page 28.

NOTE: To make the dumplings vegan, use kimchi made without fish sauce, omit the eggs, and substitute mushrooms for the pork. Finely dice 8 ounces fresh creminis and 3 to 4 fresh or reconstituted whole-cap dried medium shii-takes. After preparing the dough, preheat 1 tablespoon peanut oil in a medium skillet over medium-high heat until hot. Add all mushrooms to the pan, and cook, stirring occasionally, for 4 to 5 minutes, until they dry out and begin to stick. Set the mushrooms aside to cool, then mix them with the remaining ingredients in step 6.

NAPA KIMCHI

If I'm making kimchi, one of my favorite ferments, I'm making at least a gallon's worth, but you can scale this recipe up or down. This kimchi is largely inspired by Choi's Kimchi Company's traditional napa kimchi, my favorite commercial kimchi. I love how bright and spicy this kimchi is, and I enjoy it straight up, in all sorts of Korean dishes—especially kimchi *jjigae* (tofu stew) and kimchi *jeon* (savory pancakes)—as well as in dumpling soup (see page 147), ramen bowls, kimchi mac and cheese, and quesadillas.

NOTE: For the gochugaru, I use 1 cup coarse plus ½ cup fine. Break up any clumps before you add it to the cabbage.

MAKES 1 GALLON

- 3 medium heads napa cabbage (6½ to 7 pounds)
- 1 cup sea salt
- 1 pound daikon radish (about 1 small to medium)
- 1 to 1½ cups coarse or fine *gochugaru* (dried Korean red pepper flakes; see note)
- 5 to 6 scallions, green parts chopped into 1-inch pieces and white parts thinly sliced (about 1 cup)

- 20 cloves garlic, minced, pressed, or pulsed 15 to 20 times in a food processor (about ½ cup)
- 3 tablespoons minced or finely grated peeled fresh ginger
- 2 to 3 tablespoons fish sauce
- 1 tablespoon sugar

NOTE: I like to put the cabbage in the sink and cover it with water. Then I use a handled sieve to drain and transfer it to a 5-gallon bucket to salt it and later to mix it with the remaining ingredients. Finally, I transfer and pack it into a 1-gallon jar to ferment.

If you need a glass gallon jar, I suggest asking your local deli if they have a spare. You can also often find them at homebrew stores or in the canning supplies section of grocery and hardware stores.

1 Halve each cabbage lengthwise, remove and discard the core, then cut each half lengthwise again. Slice each section crosswise into about 1-inch-wide and 2- to 4-inch-long pieces.

2 Put the cabbage in one or two large bowls, a food-grade bucket, or your clean sink, and cover it with water to quickly rinse and soak it.

CONTINUED

3 Drain the cabbage, put it back in your container, and sprinkle it with the salt. Toss it with your hands until the cabbage is thoroughly coated, and then press it down firmly to help the cabbage release water.

4 Let the salted cabbage sit at room temperature for 4 to 5 hours, pressing it down every hour or so to help it release water.

5 Transfer the cabbage to a colander in batches, and rinse it with cold water until it tastes slightly less salty than you want your future kimchi to be. Keep in mind that you'll be adding fish sauce, which is quite salty. Gently squeeze out the excess water, and transfer the cabbage to your container.

6 Trim, peel, and halve the daikon lengthwise, and then halve each of the pieces lengthwise again. Slice all 4 pieces of daikon crosswise into ⅛- to ¼-inch-thick rounded triangles.

7 Add the daikon, gochugaru to taste, scallions, garlic, ginger, fish sauce to taste, and sugar to the cabbage, and mix thoroughly. I like to mix my kimchi (as well as a lot of dumpling fillings) by hand so that I can thoroughly blend everything and feel its texture and moisture. Note that it does leave my hands and arms a little warm for the next 30 minutes or so, even after washing all the chili off, so consider using gloves.

8 Pack the kimchi into a gallon jar or other nonreactive, lidded container. (If you have more than a gallon of kimchi, simply use another small jar for the remainder.) Push it down until the salty liquid released from the rinsed cabbage rises above the cabbage and vegetables (see note).

9 Cover the jar with a very loosely fastened lid, put the jar in a bowl or deep dish (in case it overflows), and let it sit at room temperature, away from direct sunlight, for several days. Sample the kimchi every day or so, releasing pressure from the jar as you do.

10 Fermentation time varies, but it should take 2 to 3 days to ferment in the spring or summer and up to 1 week in the fall or winter. It will get more sour, wilted, and juicy the longer it ferments. During fermentation, the kimchi will bubble and off-gas, and liquid might rise up and overflow. I keep an additional jar nearby to store the overflow liquid. I often return it to the kimchi later, when it seizes up in the refrigerator, or use it in other dishes.

11 Once the kimchi is to your liking, as zingy and tart as you want it, enjoy it and/or store it in the refrigerator for 2 to 3 months.

NOTE: Check on the kimchi every day to make sure the cabbage remains below the brine. If it doesn't, use clean hands to push it down. As kimchi ferments, pressure builds. The jar might overflow as it does. Every time you open the kimchi, pressure releases, which is a good thing. A kimchi jar once woke me in the middle of the night. It squealed every few minutes as pressure escaped. I wrapped it in a towel and carefully opened the lid. It erupted a bit as I did. Thankfully, the jar didn't shatter!

ORANGE CHICKEN

CHINA

SHAPE: Crescent

COOK: Pan-fry

SKIN: Carrot All-Purpose Egg Dough (page 42)

GARNISH: Thinly sliced scallions, or finely grated fresh orange or tangerine zest

SAUCE: Gingery Soy-Lemon (page 163) or Gyoza (page 155)

I fell hard for oranges when I was a Little League soccer player. Our team's halftime treat was quartered oranges that we'd shove in our mouths and cover our teeth with before devouring. We also got postgame sugary soda. I remember the wonderful feeling of plunging my hot little arm in the slush of half-melted cooler ice, hoping to come up with orange soda. Manners taught me to take what I got no matter what—no second tries.

These dumplings are the book's citrus celebration, using the fresh juice of an entire orange, plus lemon zest and juice in the homemade sambal. They also incorporate dried tangerine peel, or *chen pi* in Chinese, which I came across in many 1960s and '70s Chinese cookbooks during my research. For these, I took an American Chinese Hunan restaurant food staple—General Tso's chicken, invented in the 1950s in Taiwan by chef Peng Chang-kuei—and reverse-engineered it into a deliciously citrusy, soy-and-sambal-spiked chicken dumpling. Rather than frying the chicken, you fry the carroty dumpling skins encasing it.

CONTINUED →

MAKES 4½ TO 5 CUPS OF FILLING FOR 50 TO 60 DUMPLINGS

- 1½ pounds Carrot All-Purpose Egg Dough, or 60 store-bought dumpling skins
- 4 (1-inch) pieces dried tangerine peel (see page 17), or 3 tablespoons finely grated fresh orange zest (from about 1½ medium oranges)
- 2 pounds skinless, boneless chicken thighs, trimmed of visible fat and cut into 1½- to 2-inch pieces
- ½ cup freshly squeezed orange juice (from about 1 large orange)
- ¼ cup soy sauce
- 1 to 2 tablespoons homemade Sambal (page 152), or 1 tablespoon store-bought
- 2 tablespoons toasted sesame oil
- 1 tablespoon Shaoxing wine, sake, or dry sherry
- 2 tablespoons light brown sugar
- 1 tablespoon cornstarch
- 2 to 3 teaspoons kosher salt
- ½ to ¾ teaspoon freshly ground black pepper
- 3 cloves garlic, minced or pressed
- 1 (1-inch) piece peeled fresh ginger, minced or finely grated (about 1 heaping tablespoon)
- 3 to 4 scallions (both white and green parts), thinly sliced

1 Prepare the dough according to the instructions on page 42, or set out the store-bought skins.

2 Fill a small pot halfway with water, bring to a boil over high heat, and remove from the heat. Add the tangerine peel and fully submerge it under a smaller lid or plate.

3 Steep for about 30 minutes, until soft. Remove the tangerine peel from the pot and mince it.

4 Meanwhile, in the bowl of a food processor, pulse the chicken in 1 or 2 batches, 20 to 30 times per batch, until coarsely ground. (Or mince the chicken by hand into a chunky paste.)

5 In a large bowl, whisk together the orange juice, tangerine peel, soy sauce, sambal, oil, wine, sugar, cornstarch, and salt and pepper to taste.

6 Add the chicken, garlic, ginger, and scallions, and mix with your hands (gloves are fine, but I like to feel the filling) or a spoon, until all ingredients are fully and evenly incorporated. Cover and refrigerate for at least 30 minutes before using.

7 Form the dumplings according to the instructions on pages 44–46.

8 Pan-fry the dumplings according to the instructions on page 31.

NOTE: Store-bought sambal is often spicier than mine, so start with 1 tablespoon and incrementally adjust up.

DUMPLINGS = LOVE

PORK & SHRIMP SHUMAI

SHAPE: Shumai

COOK: Steam

SKIN: All-Purpose Egg Dough (page 42)

GARNISH: Finely grated or minced carrot, or thinly sliced scallions

SAUCE: Soy-Lime (page 154), Gyoza (page 155), or Chili Oil (page 150)

I've easily made shumai more than one hundred times, and no batch is ever the same. Sometimes I make the filling lighter and sweeter with more shrimp, and other times quite spicy and gingery to ward off winter colds.

The shumai from Mai Leung's 1979 cookbook *Dim Sum and Other Chinese Street Foods* were one of my gateway dumplings. I found a used copy of the cookbook in my early thirties, when I was head over heels for dim sum, and I've traveled with it tucked in my carry-on many times since. Leung was a natural-born storyteller who highly valued her culture's culinary traditions. She never missed an opportunity to educate and inspire through her books.

MAKES 4½ TO 5 CUPS OF FILLING FOR 50 TO 60 DUMPLINGS

- 1½ pounds All-Purpose Egg Dough, or 60 store-bought dumpling skins
- 5 to 6 dried whole-cap medium shiitake (black) mushrooms
- ½ pound small (51/60 count) to medium (41/50 count) shrimp, peeled and minced to a chunky paste

- 1½ pounds ground pork
- 4 to 5 scallions (both white and green parts), thinly sliced
- 1 teaspoon sugar
- 1 to 2 teaspoons kosher salt
- ¼ teaspoon freshly ground black pepper
- 1 tablespoon cornstarch

- 1 tablespoon Shaoxing wine, sake, or dry sherry
- 3 tablespoons soy sauce
- 1 to 3 tablespoons Sambal (page 152), or 1 tablespoon store-bought
- 3 tablespoons toasted sesame oil

CONTINUED ▷

1 Prepare the dough according to the instructions on page 42, or set out the store-bought skins.

2 Reconstitute the mushrooms according to the instructions on page 62 (steps 2–3), but you do not need to save and use the mushroom reconstitution water. I encourage you to keep it, though, for stocks, sauces, et cetera.

3 In a large bowl, combine the mushrooms, shrimp, pork, scallions, sugar, salt, pepper, cornstarch, wine, soy sauce, sambal, and oil. Stir vigorously, smashing and spreading with a wooden spoon, for 2 to 3 minutes, until fully blended and tacky. Cover and refrigerate for at least 30 minutes before using.

4 Form the dumplings according to the instructions on pages 44–46.

5 Steam the dumplings according to the instructions on page 28.

NOTE: Store-bought sambal is often spicier than mine, so start with 1 tablespoon and incrementally adjust up.

GARNISHING

Garnishing is a fun way to add even more character and beauty to your dumplings before or after cooking. My favorite garnishes score points for a solid combo of flavor, texture, and color: brightly colored, pop-in-your-mouth fish eggs (tobiko or salmon roe), which I add after cooking; finely grated carrot; freshly picked peas; thinly sliced scallions; thinly sliced garlic chives; thinly sliced nori; toasted black and white sesame seeds; *shichimi togarashi*; *nanami togarashi*; Chili Oil (page 150); edible flower petals; flowering herbs; and freshly roasted and ground nuts.

For 50 to 60 dumplings, aim for about ¼ cup garnish—about ⅛ to ¼ teaspoon per dumpling. Open-topped shumai (see page 22) make the most sense for garnishing, but all dumplings can benefit.

CHAWAN MUSHI EGG

JAPAN

SHAPE: XLB

COOK: Steam

SKIN: All-Purpose
Egg Dough (page
42); do not use store-
bought

GARNISH: Toasted
sesame seeds or
thinly sliced scallions

SAUCE: Soy-Lime
(page 154), Gyoza
(page 155), Sambal
(page 152), or Chili
Oil (page 150)

Japanese culinary culture honors eggs. I really appreciate how golden-orange and flavorful the yolks often are, and how expertly they're cooked in everything from ramen eggs, *tamagoyaki*, and supersoft scrambled eggs kissed with dashi, soy sauce, and sesame oil, to *chawan mushi*—a silky, tender steamed egg custard. Chawan mushi typically is about three parts stock to one part egg. I've upped the egg content here so that the dumpling filling is thick enough and holds up in the skin.

The key to these dumplings is the light, ribbony curd from cooking them slow and low. If you serve these to loved ones for brunch, I predict they'll keep your morning mug filled to the brim with hot coffee or tea forevermore.

MAKES 2½ TO 3 CUPS OF FILLING FOR 30 TO 35 DUMPLINGS

× About ¾ pound All-Purpose Egg Dough
× 3 to 4 slices bacon (see note)
× 8 large eggs
× ⅛ to ¼ teaspoon freshly ground black pepper

× ½ cup chicken or vegetable broth, or seasoned dashi (see note)
× 3 tablespoons soy sauce
× 3 tablespoons mirin or dry sherry

× 1 tablespoon toasted sesame oil
× 1 teaspoon sugar
× 2 tablespoons unsalted butter
× 3 to 4 scallions (both white and green parts), thinly sliced

CONTINUED

1 Prepare the dough according to the instructions on page 42. Do *not* use store-bought dumpling skins.

2 In a large skillet over medium heat, cook the bacon for 6 to 10 minutes, depending on thickness, until slightly crisped on the edges. Transfer to a paper-towel-lined plate to cool, then finely dice, snip with kitchen shears, or crumble.

3 In a large bowl, whisk the eggs and pepper to taste for about 1 minute, until fully combined and frothy.

4 In a small bowl, combine the broth, soy sauce, mirin, oil, and sugar, and stir until the sugar dissolves. Pour this into the eggs in a steady stream and whisk to combine.

5 In a large skillet over medium-low heat, melt the butter. Once melted, pour in the egg mixture. With a soft heatproof spatula, stir slowly and semiregularly, pulling up the curd in ribbons from the bottom and sides of the pan as it forms.

6 Cook for 3 to 4 minutes, until the eggs are very lightly set in custardy curds, still a bit wet, and slightly jiggly.

7 Add the scallions and bacon, stirring just to combine. Remove from the heat and cool to room temperature. Cover and refrigerate for at least 30 minutes before using.

8 Form the dumplings according to the instructions on pages 44–46.

9 Steam the dumplings according to the instructions on page 28.

NOTE: Bouillon cubes or paste are fine in place of the broth; if you use dashi, be sure to season to taste with salt and pepper in step 4.

To make the dumplings vegetarian, use ½ cup veggie sausage or mushrooms; if you want to substitute another protein for the bacon, use finely diced ham or shrimp. Season the preferred ingredient to taste, and sauté it in oil until fully cooked. Add it to the eggs in step 7.

I don't recommend freezing these dumplings or the filling because of the large quantity of egg. As a result, this recipe has a smaller yield than most in the book—you should serve and eat them right away.

BEEF CURRY

CHINA

SHAPE: Crescent

COOK: Pan-fry

SKIN: Curry All-Purpose Egg Dough (page 42)

GARNISH: Finely grated carrot

SAUCE: Citrusy Sambal–Sour Cream (page 160), Soy-Lime (page 154), or Gyoza (page 155)

I often have a hankering for Chinese curry puffs or hand pies—*ga li jiao* or *xian bing*—when visiting Chinese districts or markets. These wintry, warming dumplings are my way of making sure that I get to eat my version of this savory treat anytime I desire.

In Cincinnati in the 1970s and '80s, curry puffs were a popular finger food, somewhat "exotic" for the Midwest, served at well-heeled get-togethers, much like shrimp toasts or bacon-wrapped water chestnuts. If you have an old jar of curry that you're thinking of using for these, please toss it. They deserve fresh curry, and so do you.

MAKES 4½ TO 5 CUPS OF FILLING FOR 50 TO 60 DUMPLINGS

× 1½ pounds Curry All-Purpose Egg Dough, or 60 store-bought dumpling skins

× 1 medium-large russet potato (about 12 ounces)

× 3 tablespoons peanut oil, divided

× 1½ cups finely diced yellow onion (about 1 medium)

× 1½ pounds ground beef (10 to 15 percent fat, grass-fed if possible)

× 3 cloves garlic, minced or pressed

× 1 tablespoon Shaoxing wine, sake, or dry sherry

× 3 tablespoons soy sauce

× 2 to 3 teaspoons kosher salt

× 2 to 3 teaspoons sugar

× 2 tablespoons curry powder

× 1½ teaspoons ground turmeric

× 1½ teaspoons ground cumin

× 2 teaspoons red pepper flakes

× 1 to 2 tablespoons toasted sesame oil

× ¾ cup thinly sliced garlic chives

× ½ cup finely grated carrot (from about 1 medium carrot)

× 2 tablespoons freshly squeezed lime juice (from about 1 medium lime)

× 2 teaspoons finely grated lime zest (no pith; from about 1 medium lime)

CONTINUED

1 Prepare the dough according to the instructions on page 42, or set out the store-bought skins.

2 In a medium pot over high heat, cover the potato with an inch of salted water, cover it with a lid, and bring to a boil. Reduce the heat to medium and boil, partly covered, for 30 to 40 minutes, until you can easily insert a knife into the potato.

3 Cool the potato until easy to handle, and then peel it. In a large bowl, mash the potato until fairly smooth.

4 In a medium skillet over low heat, preheat 2 tablespoons of the peanut oil. Once it's hot, after 1 to 2 minutes, add the onion and cook for 10 to 12 minutes, until translucent, stirring occasionally and making sure it doesn't burn.

5 Meanwhile, in a large skillet over medium heat, preheat the remaining tablespoon of peanut oil. Once it's hot, after 1 to 2 minutes, add the beef and garlic. Cook, while completely breaking up the meat and stirring occasionally, for 3 to 4 minutes, until the meat is still pinkish but mostly cooked.

6 Increase the heat to medium high, and add the wine, soy sauce, and salt and sugar to taste. Stir to combine. Cook for 2 to 3 more minutes, until the meat is fully cooked and the pan juices have been reduced so that the meat is wet but not swimming. Transfer the beef to the bowl of mashed potato.

7 After the onion has cooked for 10 to 12 minutes, add the curry powder, turmeric, cumin, and red pepper flakes. Increase the heat to medium low, and cook for 1 to 2 minutes, stirring constantly, until the spices bloom (filling your kitchen with their sweet, spicy smell). Add the spiced onion to the bowl of mashed potato, then add the sesame oil and stir to combine.

8 Fold in the chives, carrot, and lime juice and zest, and cool to room temperature. Cover and refrigerate for at least 30 minutes before using.

9 Form the dumplings according to the instructions on pages 44–46.

10 Pan-fry the dumplings according to the instructions on page 31.

NOTE: Instead of garlic chives, you can use 4 thinly sliced scallions (both white and green parts), plus 1 minced or pressed garlic clove. You can also substitute ground pork, chicken, or shrimp for the beef.

To make the dumplings vegetarian, use 1½ pounds finely diced mushrooms in place of the beef. Cook them for 5 to 6 minutes, and then add the garlic and cook for 1 to 2 minutes more; then proceed to step 6. Reduce the amount of curry powder to 1 to 1½ tablespoons.

I don't recommend freezing these dumplings or the filling because the potato gets watery and grainy.

BEET & TURMERIC RICE *Vegan*

SHAPE: Shumai

COOK: Steam

SKIN: Beet All-Purpose Eggless Dough (page 47)

GARNISH: Toasted black sesame seeds, thinly sliced scallions, finely grated fresh ginger, or Agrumato lemon olive oil

SAUCE: Soy-Lime (page 154), Gyoza (page 155), Sambal (page 152), or Chili Oil (page 150)

I wanted to do four things with these dumplings—honor beets, which I came to appreciate later in life; shine a light on Indonesian Malaysian *nasi kunyit* or *pulut kunyit* turmeric rice (ditto); give love to vegans in dumpling form; and create a vibrant red beet skin with golden beet filling. These are one of the most beautiful dumplings in the book if you make them with beet skins (see page 52), and I highly recommend that you do.

I gave the beet skins so much attention, testing them with broths, juices, and purees. Although the skins made with all these things looked fantastic, the bite was always gummy. As a result, I recommend using powdered beets only. Drizzle these beauties in Italian Agrumato lemon olive oil before serving, and you might cry like I did when I first made them. Tears of joy.

MAKES 4½ TO 5 CUPS OF FILLING FOR 50 TO 60 DUMPLINGS

× 1½ pounds Beet All-Purpose Eggless Dough, or 60 store-bought dumpling skins

× ⅔ cup uncooked sticky rice (a.k.a. sweet/sushi/glutinous rice)

× 1 pound golden beets (about 2 medium; see note)

× 2 teaspoons ground turmeric

× 2 teaspoons butter substitute or oil of your choice

× 1 teaspoon kosher salt, divided

× 2 tablespoons freshly squeezed lemon juice (from about ½ medium lemon)

× 1 tablespoon plus 1 teaspoon toasted black sesame seeds

× 1 tablespoon plus 1 teaspoon toasted white sesame seeds

× 1 tablespoon plus 1 teaspoon peanut oil

× 2 teaspoons minced or finely grated peeled fresh ginger

× 1 teaspoon sugar

CONTINUED

1 Prepare the dough according to the instructions on page 47, or set out the store-bought skins.

2 In a medium pot, soak the rice in 1¼ cups water for 30 to 40 minutes.

3 Meanwhile, fill a medium pot three-quarters full with water and bring to a boil over high heat. Add the beets, cover partly with a lid, reduce the heat to medium, and boil for 40 to 50 minutes, until tender when pierced with a knife. Drain and cool in cold water. Peel and finely dice the beets.

4 Once the rice has soaked, add the turmeric, butter substitute, and ½ teaspoon of the salt, and bring to a boil over high heat. Stir the rice, cover the pot, reduce the heat to low, and simmer for 15 to 17 minutes, until tender.

5 Remove the rice from the heat and set aside with the lid on for 15 to 20 minutes, then fluff with a fork. Turn the rice out into a large bowl and set aside until cool enough to handle.

6 Add the beets, lemon juice, sesame seeds, oil, ginger, sugar, and the remaining ½ teaspoon salt. Mix by hand or with a wooden spoon for 1 to 2 minutes, until incorporated, being careful not to smash the beets or rice. Set aside to cool to room temperature. Cover and refrigerate for at least 30 minutes before using.

7 Form the dumplings according to the instructions on pages 44–46.

8 Steam the dumplings according to the instructions on page 28.

NOTE: You can use any beets, but golden are so sweet and tasty paired with sesame.

PORK & CABBAGE GYOZA

JAPAN

SHAPE: Crescent

COOK: Pan-fry

SKIN: All-Purpose Eggless Dough (page 47); if using store-bought skins, get gyoza skins, not wonton wrappers

GARNISH: Finely grated carrot, finely grated ginger, or thinly sliced garlic chives

SAUCE: Gyoza (page 155), Soy-Lime (page 154), Sambal (page 152), or Chili Oil (page 150)

Gabe Rosen and Kana Hinohara Hanson, co-owners of Giraffe and Noraneko in Portland, both grew up eating and loving these classic Japanese pan-fried pork-and-cabbage dumplings. When Kana was five, she already knew how to fill and form gyoza by feel. At that age, Gabe was just starting to eat them because his single dad was obsessed with Asian food and learned to make them. Nowadays, Gabe and Kana teach intimate gyoza-making classes at their Japanese food shop and café, Giraffe.

This recipe is based on Kana's mom's gyoza. While Kana was growing up, her mom would make a batch of one hundred dumplings for their family every month or so, and when she did, she enlisted her hungry kids' help. Kana said, "My brother, sister, and I would always eat as fast as we could those nights so we could get more. We'd get *really* full on gyoza nights."

MAKES 4½ TO 5 CUPS OF FILLING FOR 50 TO 60 DUMPLINGS

- 1½ pounds All-Purpose Eggless Dough, or 60 store-bought dumpling skins
- 1 pound napa cabbage (about 1 small), finely chopped

- 2 tablespoons kosher salt
- 1½ pounds ground pork
- ¾ cup chopped garlic chives (see note)
- 2½ tablespoons minced or finely grated peeled fresh ginger

- 1 tablespoon minced or pressed garlic
- 1 tablespoon soy sauce
- 1½ teaspoons toasted sesame oil
- ⅛ teaspoon freshly ground black pepper
- 1 teaspoon sugar

CONTINUED →

1 Prepare the dough according to the instructions on page 47, or set out the store-bought skins.

2 In a large bowl, combine the cabbage and salt, and roughly squeeze it for 1 to 2 minutes, until the cabbage has released liquid and wilted. You should have about 1½ cups after salting and squeezing. Set it aside for 15 to 20 minutes to continue releasing liquid.

3 In another large bowl, add the pork, chives, ginger, garlic, soy sauce, oil, pepper, and sugar, and stir until combined.

4 Drain and rinse the salted cabbage until it is the desired saltiness (most of the saltiness of the gyoza comes from the cabbage, so you want it to taste slightly oversalted on its own), and squeeze as much moisture from it as possible. Add it to the pork mixture, and mix by hand or with a spoon until thoroughly combined.

5 Cover and refrigerate for at least 30 minutes before using.

6 Form the dumplings according to the instructions on pages 44–46.

7 Pan-fry the dumplings according to the instructions on page 31.

NOTE: Instead of garlic chives, you can use 4 thinly sliced scallions (both white and green parts), plus 1 minced or pressed garlic clove.

To make the dumplings vegetarian, use 1½ pounds finely diced mushrooms in place of the pork. Sauté in oil over medium-high heat for 5 to 6 minutes, until they have softened, released much of their liquid, and the pan is fairly dry. Set aside to cool, and add to the large bowl in step 3.

COCONUT-SESAME *Vegetarian*

VIETNAM

SHAPE: Shumai

COOK: Steam

SKIN: Charcoal-Sesame All-Purpose Egg Dough (page 42) or Gluten-Free Rice Flour Dough (page 49)

GARNISH: Toasted, shredded unsweetened coconut, or toasted black or white sesame seeds

SAUCE: None

I tried *bo bia ngot*, a sweet summer wrap, for the first time while on an all-day food tour in Hanoi with a young Vietnamese woman named Miss Moon. During the tour, she took off running to flag down an older man on a bicycle. He opened a bin on the back of his cruiser, pulled out a cutting board, and topped a paper-thin rice crepe with crunchy spun sugarcane sticks. Then he shaved thinly grated fresh coconut over it and gave everything a few strong shakes of toasted black sesame seeds before rolling it up. It's one of the best desserts I've ever had.

Afterward, Miss Moon told me that this deaf and mute man biked to town daily to peddle bo bia ngot. He sold very little because most tourists thought he was peddling beer—*bia* in Vietnamese. These dumplings are in honor of that man, his perseverance, and his deliciously sweet toasty treats.

MAKES 4½ TO 5 CUPS OF FILLING FOR 50 TO 60 DUMPLINGS

- 1½ pounds Charcoal-Sesame All-Purpose Egg Dough or Gluten-Free Rice Flour Dough, or 60 store-bought dumpling skins
- ¾ cup untoasted black sesame seeds
- ¾ cup untoasted white sesame seeds
- 2 cups shredded unsweetened coconut, divided
- ¾ cup honey
- ½ cup light brown sugar
- 1 cup sesame paste or tahini, with some of its oil
- ¼ teaspoon kosher salt

CONTINUED

1 Prepare the dough according to the instructions on page 42 or 49, respectively, or set out the store-bought skins. I recommend using smaller 3- to 3½-inch skins for these since they are rich and sweet like candy.

2 In a large skillet over medium-low heat, toast the sesame seeds for 4 to 5 minutes, stirring occasionally and making sure that they don't burn, until the white sesame seeds are golden and aromatic. The shift happens very quickly: the seeds will start to snap and crackle, and you might get a touch of smoke. Once they are golden, remove them from the heat immediately because if they toast too long, they'll become dark and bitter. Transfer them to a baking sheet in an even layer to cool.

3 In a small skillet over medium-low heat, toast ¼ cup of the coconut for 3 to 4 minutes, stirring occasionally and making sure that it doesn't burn, until it has turned golden. This shift also happens quickly, so be careful not to burn it. Transfer it to a plate or shallow bowl to cool for later use as garnish.

4 In a medium pot over medium-low heat, warm the honey, sugar, and sesame paste for 3 to 4 minutes, stirring regularly, until the sugar has mostly dissolved but is still slightly grainy. Remove from the heat.

5 In a food processor or coffee grinder, or using a mortar and pestle, coarsely grind the cooled sesame seeds.

6 In a medium bowl, combine the remaining 1¾ cups coconut, the ground sesame seeds, and the salt, and slowly stir in the still-warm honey mixture. Work it together with your hands. This feels a bit like kneading a sticky, grainy dough. Use while still slightly warm and malleable.

7 Form the dumplings according to the instructions on pages 44–46 or 51, respectively.

8 Steam the dumplings according to the instructions on page 28 or 30, respectively.

NOTE: If you can't find untoasted sesame seeds, don't worry, use toasted and simply halve the toasting time in step 2.

As the filling cools, it stiffens, so cover it to keep it warm and workable. If you refrigerate it for later use, microwave it in 10-second bursts for 40 to 50 seconds total, stirring between each burst.

If you don't use all the filling, make yummy sesame bar candies: lightly grease a shallow baking dish, press the filling in, cover, and refrigerate. Once the candy has chilled, slice it into small pieces. It's also tasty crumbled over yogurt, granola, and ice cream.

XLB, A.K.A. SOUP DUMPLINGS

The first time I had soup dumplings, known in China as xiao long bao, or XLB, was several years ago in Seattle, where I hunted them down. I'd heard tell of their magic, and they did not disappoint. The secret to soup dumplings is the cubed broth that looks and behaves very similarly to Jell-O: it sets loosely at room temperature, firmly when chilled, and liquefies when heated. It feels like magic but, of course, it's good old kitchen science. You can make a lot of the dumplings in this book into XLB by adding cubed broth or water to them, including Mapo Tofu (page 102), Cincinnati Chili (page 118), Salmon-Sesame (page 63), Orange Chicken (page 73), and Pork & Shrimp Shumai (page 75).

Soup dumplings are usually meaty, so non–meat eaters miss out. For this book, I wanted to use an alternative to animal-based gelatin or slow-simmered pork skin and bones for firming up the broth—algae-derived agar-agar powder won (see page 94). Now vegetarians, vegans, and pescatarians can have their yummy fun with XLB too!

I have created three very tasty XLB recipes, and they all are fairly flexible in terms of ingredients. Once you get the agar-agar broth cubes down, you'll see how easy these are to put together. Basically, you firm up a broth with agar-agar, cube it, and mix it into your filling. When the cubed broth is steamed within the dumpling, it beautifully melts back into broth. Please only freeze XLB in dumpling form; the filling or cubes on their own will "sweat" significantly.

A NOTE ABOUT SKIN THICKNESS: Roll XLB skins slightly thicker than your average dumpling skin, to about ⅛ inch. You can use ¹⁄₁₆-inch skins, but I don't recommend trying that until you've mastered them with ⅛ inch. Do *not* use store-bought skins for XLB—they are not pliable enough.

I like to cook and serve XLB in lightly oiled tartlet molds or Asian soup spoons. That way, if the skin breaks at any point during steaming or serving, you don't lose the precious broth. In a pinch, you can steam the XLB in pieces of aluminum foil fashioned into small cups. Obviously, just be sure that whatever you use is heatproof. There is no right or wrong way to eat XLB, but I usually grab mine from the soup spoon or tartlet mold with chopsticks, and bite or poke a small hole in the top or side. I slurp up the filling, or if it's too hot, I squeeze the dumpling with my chopsticks so that the broth spills into the spoon or mold to cool. Some people, especially kids, like to stick wide, short drinking straws into the top of XLB to suck up the broth.

MAKING AGAR-AGAR BROTH OR WATER

If you've ever made Jell-O, making agar-agar cubes for soup dumplings will feel very familiar. I recommend using agar-agar powder to make cubed broth or water because it's most reliable. For each ½ cup of salted water or broth, add ½ teaspoon of agar-agar powder, 1½ teaspoons of flakes, or a 1-inch piece of stick. The sticks take longer to break down, so I recommend chopping them up first and cooking them for 1 or 2 minutes longer, until fully dissolved.

TESTING THE CUBES: Before adding the cubes to a dumpling filling, always test one by cooking it for 1 to 2 minutes in an Asian soup spoon, tartlet mold, or ramekin placed in a steamer to make sure it dissolves properly. If it does not, discard the batch and start a new one.

KEEPING THE CUBES COOL: The cubes sweat and release liquid if they get too warm, so keep out only a cup or so of XLB filling at a time as you fill the dumplings. Keep the rest of the filling refrigerated until you are ready to use it.

FOR BROTH

× 2½ cups flavorful homemade or good-quality store-bought broth
× 2½ teaspoons agar-agar powder

FOR WATER

× ½ cup water
× ½ teaspoon agar-agar powder

1 In a medium pot if using broth, or a small pot if using water, over high heat, bring the liquid to a boil. Reduce the heat to a light simmer, add the agar-agar, and whisk continuously for 1 to 3 minutes, until it is fully dissolved.

2 Strain the broth or water through a fine-mesh sieve into a 9-by-13-inch pan if using broth, or an 8-inch-square pan if using water (or a similarly sized heatproof dish). Cool the broth or water at room temperature for 15 to 20 minutes, until partially set. Transfer it to the refrigerator to chill, uncovered, until fully set, for 20 to 30 minutes if using broth, or 10 to 15 minutes if using water.

3 Remove from the refrigerator, and thinly slice it with a thin butter knife into the smallest cubes possible—aim for about ⅛ inch, but there is no need to be precise in size or shape. Do your best; it's very jiggly. Slice it in one direction, and then turn the pan 90 degrees and slice it in the opposite direction to make tiny cubes. Return the cubes to the refrigerator, uncovered, for up to 2 hours, or tightly cover and refrigerate for up to 2 days. I do not recommend freezing the cubes unless they are already formed into soup dumplings because they get freezer burn easily on their own and sweat significantly when defrosting.

PORK XLB

SHAPE: XLB

COOK: Steam

SKIN: All Purpose Eggless Dough (page 47) or All-Purpose Egg Dough (page 42); do not use store-bought

GARNISH: None

SAUCE: Black vinegar with julienned or shredded fresh ginger (traditional accompaniment), Gingery Soy-Lemon (page 163), or Sambal (page 152)

Pork XLB is the most ubiquitous type of soup dumpling in American restaurants, and they deserve the spotlight. When I serve a medley of dumplings, these always rank very highly. They are classic dumpling comfort food, plumped up with brothy ground pork (substitute ground chicken or beef if you prefer) and loaded with ginger and scallions.

According to cookbook author Andrea Nguyen, in her book *Asian Dumplings*, soup dumplings were invented in the late 1800s in a Naxiang village outside of Shanghai. I'm so glad that in the hundred-plus years that followed, they made their way to America.

MAKES ABOUT 5 CUPS OF FILLING FOR 50 TO 60 DUMPLINGS

- 1½ pounds All-Purpose Eggless Dough or All-Purpose Egg Dough
- 2½ cups agar-agar broth (see page 94)
- 3 tablespoons soy sauce
- 2 tablespoons Shaoxing wine, sake, or dry sherry

- 1½ tablespoons toasted sesame oil
- 2 to 3 teaspoons sugar
- 1 to 3 teaspoons kosher salt
- ½ to 1 teaspoon freshly ground black pepper

- 1¼ pounds finely chopped or ground pork
- 4 to 5 scallions (both white and green parts), thinly sliced
- 1 tablespoon minced or finely grated peeled fresh ginger

1 Prepare the dough according to the instructions on page 47 or 42, respectively. Do *not* use store-bought dumpling skins.

2 Prepare the agar-agar broth according to the instructions on page 94.

3 In a large bowl, combine the soy sauce, wine, oil, and sugar, salt, and pepper to taste. Stir until the salt and sugar have dissolved.

4 Add the pork, scallions, and ginger, and mix by hand or with a wooden spoon until fully incorporated. Cover and refrigerate for at least 30 minutes before using.

5 If any liquid has sweated out, transfer the broth cubes to a fine-mesh sieve and let it drain for 30 seconds, then add the cubes to the chilled pork mixture. Stir with a wooden spoon until the broth cubes are evenly distributed.

6 Form the dumplings according to the instructions on pages 44–46.

7 Steam the dumplings according to the instructions on page 28.

SHRIMP XLB

CHINA

SHAPE: XLB

COOK: Steam

SKIN: All Purpose Eggless Dough (page 47) or All-Purpose Egg Dough (page 42); do not use store-bought

GARNISH: None

SAUCE: Black vinegar with julienned or shredded fresh ginger (traditional accompaniment), Gingery Soy-Lemon (page 163), or Sambal (page 152)

Shrimp is one of my all-time favorite dumpling fillings—I love how sweet, juicy, and tender they are when cooked properly. It's also beautiful to have that bright pink interior peeking through a pale dumpling skin. As with the pork and mushroom XLB, this recipe is deceptively simple. Din Tai Fung, the world-renowned Taiwanese soup dumpling and noodle chain, has played a large part in making XLB so popular worldwide. I love their shrimp and angled gourd (a.k.a. luffa or silk squash) XLB. And it's always fun to peek into their partly exposed kitchen and watch as the cooks expertly pleat and form the dumplings.

MAKES ABOUT 5 CUPS OF FILLING FOR 50 TO 60 DUMPLINGS

- 1½ pounds All-Purpose Eggless Dough or All-Purpose Egg Dough
- 2½ cups agar-agar broth (page 94)
- 3 tablespoons soy sauce
- 2 tablespoons Shaoxing wine, sake, or dry sherry
- 1½ tablespoons toasted sesame oil

- 2 to 3 teaspoons sugar
- 1 to 3 teaspoons kosher salt
- ½ to 1 teaspoon freshly ground black pepper
- 1¼ pounds small (51/60 count) to medium (41/50 count) shrimp, peeled and finely chopped

- 4 to 5 scallions (both white and green parts), thinly sliced
- 1 tablespoon minced or finely grated peeled fresh ginger

1 Prepare the dough according to the instructions on page 47 or 42, respectively. Do *not* use store-bought dumpling skins.

2 Prepare the agar-agar broth according to the instructions on page 94.

3 In a large bowl, combine the soy sauce, wine, oil, and the sugar, salt, and pepper to taste. Stir until the salt and sugar have dissolved.

4 Add the shrimp, scallions, and ginger and mix by hand or with a wooden spoon until fully incorporated. Cover and refrigerate for at least 30 minutes before using.

5 If any liquid has sweated out, transfer the broth cubes to a fine-mesh sieve and let them drain for 30 seconds, then add the cubes to the chilled shrimp mixture. Stir with a wooden spoon until the broth cubes are evenly distributed.

6 Form the dumplings according to the instructions on pages 44–46.

7 Steam the dumplings according to the instructions on page 28.

MUSHROOM XLB *Vegan*

CHINA

SHAPE: XLB

COOK: Steam

SKIN: All-Purpose Eggless Dough (page 47); do not use store-bought

GARNISH: None

SAUCE: Black vinegar with julienned or shredded fresh ginger (traditional accompaniment), Gingery Soy-Lemon (page 163), or Sambal (page 152)

One of my goals early on with this cookbook was to develop a vegan soup dumpling. Vegans usually miss out on XLB when dining out since pork is the most common filling. I want everyone to be able to enjoy the brothy comfort of these gorgeous gingery dumplings. Feel free to substitute a different type of mushroom here. Simply cook them until they are toothsome and well seasoned, and the pan is fairly dry. You can also substitute another minced vegetable that has a nice, tender bite. I recommend starting with mushrooms and then branching out.

MAKES ABOUT 5 CUPS OF FILLING FOR 50 TO 60 DUMPLINGS

- 1½ pounds All-Purpose Eggless Dough
- 2½ cups agar-agar broth (page 94)
- 4 to 6 dried whole-cap medium shiitake (black) mushrooms
- 1 pound fresh cremini or button mushrooms, finely diced
- 2 tablespoons peanut oil
- 3 tablespoons soy sauce
- 2 tablespoons Shaoxing wine, sake, or dry sherry
- 2 to 3 teaspoons sugar
- 1 to 3 teaspoons kosher salt
- ½ to 1 teaspoon freshly ground black pepper
- 1½ tablespoons toasted sesame oil
- 4 to 5 scallions (both white and green parts), thinly sliced
- 1 tablespoon minced or finely grated peeled fresh ginger

1 Prepare the dough according to the instructions on page 47. Do *not* use store-bought dumpling skins.

2 Prepare the agar-agar broth according to the instructions on page 94.

3 Reconstitute the dried mushrooms according to the instructions on page 62 (steps 2–3).

4 Meanwhile, in a large skillet over medium-high heat, preheat the peanut oil. Once it's hot, after 1 to 2 minutes, add both types of mushrooms and cook for 1 to 2 minutes, or until they begin to soften, stirring occasionally.

5 Add the soy sauce, wine, and ½ cup of the reserved mushroom water, and cook for 6 to 8 minutes, stirring occasionally, until the pan is fairly dry.

6 Add the sugar, salt, and pepper to taste, and the sesame oil, scallions, and ginger, and cook for 1 to 2 minutes, until incorporated. Remove from the heat and cool until the mixture is no longer steaming, stirring occasionally to cool it faster. Cover and refrigerate for at least 30 minutes before using.

7 If any liquid has sweated out, transfer the broth cubes to a fine-mesh sieve and let them drain for 30 seconds, then add the cubes to the chilled mushroom mixture. Stir with a wooden spoon until the broth cubes are evenly distributed.

8 Form the dumplings according to the instructions on pages 44–46.

9 Steam the dumplings according to the instructions on page 28.

MAPO TOFU

CHINA

SHAPE: XLB

COOK: Steam

SKIN: Black Sesame
All-Purpose Egg
Dough (page 42); do
not use store-bought

GARNISH: Thinly
sliced scallions

SAUCE: Black vinegar
or straight up

Mapo tofu is chock-full of ferments, loaded with a numbing amount of Sichuan peppercorn, and texturally pleasing. I love its combo of silky tofu and ground pork so much that I almost always have to order it when I see it on a menu.

Since Chinese culinary culture is integral to dumplings, I tried my hand at fermenting *doubanjiang*—the chunky, spicy Sichuan fermented fava bean chili paste that is a key ingredient in mapo tofu. It's super tasty: think miso with a kick. It's also fairly easy to find at Asian markets.

MAKES 4½ TO 5 CUPS OF FILLING FOR 50 TO 60 DUMPLINGS

- 1½ pounds Black Sesame All-Purpose Egg Dough
- ½ cup agar-agar water (page 94)
- 2 tablespoons doubanjiang
- 1½ tablespoons soy sauce
- 1 tablespoon mashed fermented black beans or miso
- 1 tablespoon Shaoxing wine, sake, or dry sherry
- 2 teaspoons sugar
- ¼ to ½ teaspoon cayenne

- ¼ to ½ teaspoon kosher salt
- 1 tablespoon peanut oil
- ¾ pound ground pork
- 2 teaspoons minced or finely grated peeled fresh ginger
- 3 cloves garlic, minced or pressed
- 1 (14- to 16-ounce) block soft tofu, cut into ½-inch cubes
- ½ cup flavorful homemade or good-quality store-bought broth (bouillon cubes or paste are fine too)

- 2 tablespoons cornstarch
- 3 tablespoons water
- 2 to 3 scallions (both white and green parts), thinly sliced
- 1 to 2 teaspoons finely ground Sichuan peppercorn
- 1½ teaspoons toasted sesame oil

CONTINUED

1 Prepare the dough according to the instructions on page 42. Do *not* use store-bought dumpling skins.

2 Prepare the agar-agar water according to the instructions on page 94.

3 In a small bowl, stir together the doubanjiang, soy sauce, fermented black beans, wine, sugar, cayenne, and salt to taste.

4 In a large skillet over medium heat, preheat the peanut oil. Once it's hot, after 1 to 2 minutes, add the pork and cook for 2 to 3 minutes while breaking it up, until the pork is mostly cooked and just slightly pinkish.

5 Add the ginger and garlic and cook for about 1 minute, until fragrant. Add the doubanjiang mixture, and cook for 1 to 2 minutes, stirring constantly, until incorporated. Add the tofu, gently stirring so as not to break it up, and reduce the heat to low. Add the broth, cover, and very lightly simmer for 2 to 3 minutes, until the tofu plumps up and the sauce thickens slightly.

6 In a small bowl, combine the cornstarch and water, and stir until the cornstarch has dissolved. Add the scallions and cornstarch water to the pork-tofu mixture, and stir gently and constantly for 1 to 2 minutes, until the sauce has thickened.

7 Add the Sichuan peppercorn and sesame oil and gently stir to combine. Remove from the heat and cool to room temperature. Cover and refrigerate for at least 30 minutes before using.

8 If any water has sweated out of the agar-agar water cubes, transfer them to a fine-mesh sieve and let them drain for 30 seconds, then gently stir them with a wooden spoon into the chilled mapo tofu until the cubes are evenly distributed.

9 Form the dumplings according to the instructions on pages 44–46.

10 Steam the dumplings according to the instructions on page 28.

NOTE: If you're making this as a stand-alone dish served with rice, and not for a dumpling filling, use ¾ cup broth instead of ½ cup; it will make 3 to 4 servings. You can also make this recipe without the agar-agar water, chill it, and then form the dumplings. The filling will be thicker and not as soupy.

To make the dumplings vegetarian, finely dice ¾ pound fresh shiitake, cremini, or button mushrooms (or a combination), and add them to the pan in place of the pork with 1 additional tablespoon of peanut oil. Cook them for 5 to 6 minutes, stirring occasionally, until they are fairly dry, and proceed with the recipe as written.

HISTORY OF DUMPLINGS

There are many origin theories when it comes to dumplings, but the most favored and often cited celebrates Zhang Zhongjing, the founder of Chinese herbal medicine. Zhongjing lived in China during the Han dynasty (206 BCE to 220 CE), when the flour mill was introduced to China and rice and wheat flour became prevalent. He worked as a government official in Changsha in the Hunan province, while treating sick and suffering folks with boiled herb broths on the side.

One year, as the story goes, during a devastating regional outbreak of typhoid in the winter, Zhongjing set up shop in front of his government building, put a large pot to boil, and got to work treating locals, many of whom suffered from frostbitten and decaying ears. He boiled mutton with healing herbs, chopped that all up, and wrapped it in wheat-flour skins, shaping his creations like ears before boiling them.

Those who ate Zhongjing's medicine—supposedly the world's first dumplings—felt warmth quickly return to their bodies and improved overall health. They celebrated their swift recoveries and rang in that auspicious new year not long after with their own dumpling renditions.

After that, dumpling making spread throughout northern China and became a winter-into-spring tradition, particularly during Chinese New Year celebrations and festivals.

Recently, archaeologists unearthed three dumplings from Xinjiang Uygur in China and determined them to have been made at some point between the third and sixth centuries! This serves to remind us that although the word *dumpling* is only a few hundred years old, dumplings themselves are thousands of years old.

I appreciate the core message of the Zhongjing dumpling story: Love your fellow humans. Care for them always, particularly when they are suffering, and nurture them with handmade, healing food.

DUMPLINGS BEYOND ASIA

Most cultures lay claim to at least one type of dumpling, whatever definition of dumpling you subscribe to, and what follows are some of my favorites from eastern Europe, Norway, and beyond that are especially worth a try.

Some of the regional recipes in this chapter come directly from people I love, such as the Norwegian Potato Komper and the Goat Cheese Arrabbiata, while others are my own creations inspired by my woodsy and forage-friendly Pacific Northwest home, my Midwest upbringing, my travels, or a combination of all three. There were so many potential recipes that ultimately didn't make it into the book—including Native American grape dumplings, Ethiopian chickpea dumplings, and Turkish *manti*—but they are absolutely worth seeking out.

I often get asked if I ever grow tired of dumplings, and the answer is a resounding no. There is simply too much diversity in the wide world of dumplings. The testing and development phase was a very creative and all-purpose-flour-covered time for me that I will always remember fondly. I hope you get inspired and have just as much fun making these dumplings yourself. Remember, there are no rules.

MOREL-SHERRY CREAM *Vegetarian*

NORTHWEST US

SHAPE: Shumai

COOK: Steam

SKIN: Smoked Paprika All-Purpose Eggless Dough (page 47)

GARNISH: Before steaming, top each dumpling with 1 thinly sliced round of reconstituted morel. Or, also before steaming, place 1 skinny 2- to 2½-inch asparagus top into each dumpling so that it sticks out as if growing from inside.

SAUCE: Citrusy Sambal–Sour Cream (page 160), Sambal (page 152), Chili Oil (page 150), or Agrumato lemon olive oil

The gate to mushroom foraging opened for me when I moved to Portland. Since then, I've hunted for all sorts of mushrooms, including morels, boletes (porcini), and chanterelles. Morels are my favorite. I admire their conical honeycomb shape, strong woodsy umami, the way they grow in the duff, their mettle (spreading spores rapidly in burn zones), and how they're—strangely enough—often better dried and reconstituted than fresh.

I've been lucky enough to take part a few times in a Pacific Northwest spring morel-hunting campout with friends called Morel Madness. Once we collect the morel mother lode, we make a huge batch of rich and buttery campfire morel cream sauce. I can *never* get enough. This recipe is in honor of that. If you forage for morels and then cook these dumplings with them, I bet you'll catch a bit of the madness too.

If you want a full foraging feast, these go really well with the Nettle & Caramelized Onion dumplings (page 113).

CONTINUED >

MAKES 4½ TO 5 CUPS OF FILLING FOR 50 TO 60 DUMPLINGS

- 1½ pounds Smoked Paprika All-Purpose Eggless Dough, or 60 store-bought dumpling skins
- ⅔ cup long-grain rice
- 1⅓ cup water
- 3 cups whole dried morels (about 3 ounces)
- 2 tablespoons unsalted butter
- 2 tablespoons extra-virgin olive oil

- 4 cloves garlic, minced or pressed
- 1½ cups heavy cream
- ¼ cup dry sherry, Shaoxing wine, or sake
- 1 tablespoon smoked paprika
- 1½ to 2½ teaspoons kosher salt
- 1 teaspoon freshly ground black pepper

- 1 tablespoon rinsed, minced preserved lemon (about 1 lemon quarter; recipe follows), pith removed and discarded, or 3 tablespoons finely grated fresh lemon zest
- ¼ cup freshly squeezed lemon juice (from about 1 medium lemon)
- 4 to 5 scallions (both white and green parts), thinly sliced

1   Prepare the dough according to the instructions on page 47, or set out the store-bought skins.

2   In a small pot, combine the rice and water, and bring to a boil over of high heat. Stir the rice, cover the pot, reduce the heat to low, and simmer for 15 to 17 minutes.

3   Remove the rice from the heat and set aside with the lid on for 10 minutes, then fluff with a fork. Turn the rice out into a large bowl.

4   Meanwhile, reconstitute the morels in 3 cups water according to the instructions on page 62 (steps 2–3). Thinly slice them if they are small or medium, finely dice if large.

5   In a medium skillet over medium heat, melt the butter, and then add the oil, garlic, and morels. (If desired, reserve ¼ cup of the sliced morels for topping the dumplings prior to steaming.) Cook for 1 to 2 minutes, stirring occasionally, until the morels begin to soften.

6   Add ½ cup of the reserved mushroom water and simmer for 2 to 3 minutes, until the water has reduced by about half.

7   Add the cream, sherry, paprika, salt to taste, and pepper. Bring to a simmer, then reduce the heat to medium low and lightly simmer for 12 to 15 minutes, stirring occasionally, until the sauce has reduced by about one-third.

NOTE: Instead of dried morels, you could use 1 pound whole fresh morels, or other wild or cremini mushrooms. Cook fresh mushrooms for 5 to 7 minutes, until they have released their juices and most of the liquid has evaporated. Add the garlic and cook for 1 minute. Skip step 6.

8 Add the preserved lemon, lemon juice, and scallions, and cook for 3 to 4 minutes, until the scallions begin to soften.

9 Add the sauce to the cooked rice, stir to combine, and cool to room temperature. The filling should be a bit wet and the consistency of risotto. The rice will continue to absorb the sauce as it cools. Once it is room temperature, cover and refrigerate for at least 30 minutes before using.

10 Form the dumplings according to the instructions on pages 44–46.

11 Steam the dumplings according to the instructions on page 28.

PRESERVED LEMONS

Almost every time I use these in a dish, rinsed and minced, someone will ask me, "What makes this so delicious?" Preserved lemons! They have everything that you love about lemons without the acid. I first learned how to make them from my favorite chef, John Gorham, for our Spanish cookbook, *Toro Bravo*.

I often add preserved lemon to deviled eggs, salad dressings, tuna and chicken salad, pasta dishes like orzo salad, grilled salmon, and well, you guessed it, dumplings. Please be conservative with them, though. Like truffle oil or garlic, if you add too much, they can overpower everything else.

MAKES 1 QUART

× 3 to 4 medium lemons
× 1½ cups kosher salt

× ¼ to ⅓ cup freshly squeezed lemon juice (from about 1 medium lemon)
× ¼ to ⅓ cup water

CONTINUED >

1 Clean the lemons, remove the ends, and quarter them. Discard the easy-to-remove seeds.

2 Pour a thin layer of salt in the bottom of a quart jar. Layer three or four lemon quarters over it, add salt to cover, and continue layering lemons and salt. Push down on and pack the lemons into the jar as you do, either by hand or with a heavy pestle or wooden spoon. Reserve enough salt to cover them at the end.

3 After the final lemons have been covered in salt, pour in the lemon juice and water. You want the juicy slurry to get to about 1 inch from the top of the jar. Add more water if necessary.

4 Wrap the jar in a towel and store it in a cool, dark spot for 6 weeks. Check on it a few times, and add more water and salt if the lemons become exposed. After the 6 weeks, refrigerate for up to 3 months.

NOTE: When cooking with preserved lemons, give them a good rinse to get rid of the salt. Remove and discard the flesh (or rinse it as well and use in stews or braises) and scrape off and discard the white pith. I do this with the back of a spoon. What's left is the bright-tasting, preserved yellow skin and all its lemony goodness.

NETTLE & CARAMELIZED ONION *Vegetarian*

The first time I encountered nettles, I was helping cultivate them on a small, organic culinary herb farm in Spain. I had tingly arms, hands, and legs for most of my months there. It was worth it though, because I got to eat nettles! The farm's owner, Julia, prepared them simply—sautéed for a flash in the pan with deliciously fruity local Manzanilla olive oil.

I forage for nettles every spring through summer now. In addition to making these dumplings, I like to simply sauté nettles, steep them fresh or dried for tea, make pesto, and dehydrate and grind them into nettle powder for dumpling skins. These flavor-packed dumplings marry nettles with sweetly complex caramelized onions and the Pacific Northwest's most beloved nut, the hazelnut (a.k.a. filbert).

MAKES 4½ TO 5 CUPS OF FILLING FOR 50 TO 60 DUMPLINGS

- 1½ pounds Nettle All-Purpose Egg Dough, or 60 store-bought dumpling skins
- ½ to 1 teaspoon kosher salt, plus more for blanching
- 1 cup raw hazelnuts
- 4 packed cups fresh stinging nettle leaves (about ¼ pound)
- ½ cup olive or peanut oil (see note)
- 2 medium yellow onions, thinly sliced (about 4 cups)
- ½ cup Shaoxing wine, sake, or dry sherry
- 1½ cups crumbled feta cheese (about 6 ounces)
- Freshly squeezed juice of ½ medium lemon (about 2 tablespoons)

CONTINUED ▷

1 Prepare the dough according to the instructions on page 42, or set out the store-bought skins.

2 Prepare an ice-water bath in a large bowl. Fill a large pot with lightly salted water and bring to a boil over high heat.

3 Meanwhile, in a medium skillet over medium-high heat, toast the hazelnuts for 5 to 7 minutes, stirring or shaking the pan occasionally, until the nuts are a darker brown, fragrant, and toasted. Remove from the heat, cool, and finely chop.

4 Once the water is boiling, add the nettles and blanch for exactly 30 seconds. (An easy way to do this is to put the nettle leaves in a handled sieve that you can lower into the water and quickly remove when done.)

5 Remove the nettles, let them drain, and cool them in the ice-water bath. Squeeze out the moisture, dice, and then fluff with your hands and pull apart all the leaves. The sting has now been completely deactivated, so it is safe to use your hands.

6 In a large skillet over medium-low heat, preheat the oil until hot. Then add the onions and cook, stirring occasionally, for 12 to 15 minutes, until they are lightly golden, soft, and translucent.

7 Add the salt to taste, reduce the heat to low, and continue cooking for 20 to 25 more minutes, stirring occasionally and being careful not to burn the onions, until they are golden brown and caramelized. The longer you cook them, the more flavorful they'll be.

8 Add the wine, stir to combine, increase the heat to medium-low, and simmer for 8 to 10 minutes.

9 Add the cooked nettles, stir to combine, and cook for 2 to 3 minutes, just to incorporate.

10 Sprinkle the feta over the top, reduce the heat to low, and cook for 2 to 3 minutes, until the feta softens. Do not stir. Add the toasted hazelnuts and lemon juice, and stir to combine. Set aside to cool to room temperature. Cover and refrigerate for at least 30 minutes before using.

11 Form the dumplings according to the instructions on pages 44–46.

12 Pan-fry the dumplings according to the instructions on page 31.

NOTE: Be careful when handling nettles! I wear long rubber dish-washing gloves when de-stemming them and use tongs when cooking. Brief heat deactivates the formic acid and chemicals in the plant's hair-like needles that cause the stinging sensation.

NOTE: If you are serving these dumplings with nettle pesto, cook them in olive oil; if serving with a soy sauce–based dipping sauce, then use peanut oil. For a full foraging feast, pair them with the Morel–Sherry Cream dumplings (page 108).

To make the dumplings vegan, use All-Purpose Eggless Dough (page 47) and simply omit the feta or use a vegan substitute.

CONTINUED →

NETTLE PESTO

I usually grow a healthy amount of arugula in my garden, and in the spring and summer I collect grips of nettles. Both flavorful greens have what it takes to stand up to pesto's strong showing of garlic, and they're always thirsty for a healthy glug or two of olive oil. This recipe scales up perfectly, by the way.

I enjoy nettle pesto paired with pasta dishes, particularly orzo with preserved lemons (see page 111), slathered on salmon before cooking, and spread on freshly buttered toast or garlic bread. It's also great spooned into various cold meat or fish salads with mayonnaise.

MAKES ABOUT 1 CUP

- × ¼ to ½ teaspoon kosher salt, plus more for blanching
- × ⅓ cup raw hazelnuts
- × 1½ cups packed fresh stinging nettle leaves (see note on page 115), or 2 cups packed stemmed arugula (see note on page 117)
- × 4 cloves garlic
- × ½ cup extra-virgin olive oil
- × Freshly squeezed juice of ¼ to ½ medium lemon (1 to 2 tablespoons)
- × ½ cup finely grated Asiago cheese (about 1 ounce)
- × ⅛ teaspoon freshly ground black pepper

1   Prepare an ice-water bath in a large bowl. Fill a large pot with lightly salted water and bring to a boil.

2   Meanwhile, in a small skillet over medium–high heat, toast the hazelnuts for 5 to 7 minutes, stirring or shaking the pan occasionally, until the nuts are a darker brown, fragrant, and toasted. Remove from the heat to cool.

3   Once the water is boiling, add the nettles and blanch for exactly 30 seconds. (An easy way to do this is to put the nettles in a handled sieve that you can lower into the water and remove quickly when done.)

4   Remove the nettles, let them drain, and cool them in the ice-water bath. Squeeze out the moisture, coarsely chop them, and then fluff with your hands and pull apart all the leaves.

5   In the bowl of a food processor or blender, add the nettles, garlic, and hazelnuts. Pulse 30 to 40 times, while slowly and steadily adding the oil and lemon juice, until smooth and creamy. Scrape down the sides with a spatula once or twice. Add the cheese and salt and pepper to taste. Serve or refrigerate in an airtight container for up to 1 week.

NOTE: If making this pesto with arugula, skip the blanching step. Toast and cool the hazelnuts as directed, then proceed to step 5.

CINCINNATI CHILI

MIDWEST US

SHAPE: XLB

COOK: Steam

SKIN: All-Purpose Eggless Dough (page 47); do not use store-bought

GARNISH: Oyster crackers

SAUCE: Frank's Original RedHot

I developed these dumplings with my then-six- and eight-year-old nieces Hannah and Marielle when I was home in Cincinnati for the holidays. Since the 1920s, Cincinnati chili has been a regional American specialty with Greek and Macedonian roots. It is my family's tradition to cook and serve it buffet-style for Christmas Eve dinner. I decided to come up with a dumpling version since I always make dumplings over the holidays as well.

It was a revelation. Noodle on the outside, chili and cheese on the inside! They were essentially tiny three-ways (see page 123). Everyone loved them and a new tradition was born.

MAKES 4½ TO 5 CUPS OF FILLING FOR 50 TO 60 DUMPLINGS

- × 1½ pounds All-Purpose Eggless Dough
- × About 4 cups Crain Family Chili (recipe follows)

OPTIONAL FILLINGS
- × ¼ to ½ cup finely diced yellow onion
- × ¼ to ½ cup canned kidney or red beans
- × ½ to 1 cup finely grated sharp cheddar cheese (1 to 2 ounces)

- × ½ to 1 cup finely diced hot dog or veggie dog (1 to 2 hot dogs)
- × 3 to 4 tablespoons Frank's Original RedHot
- × 3 to 4 tablespoons yellow mustard

1 Prepare the dough according to the instructions on page 47. Do *not* use store-bought skins.

2 Prepare the chili according to the instructions on page 122.

3 Fill each skin with 2 heaping teaspoons of the chilled chili, plus any combination of the optional fillings.

4 Form the dumplings according to instructions on pages 44–46.

5 Steam the dumplings according to the instructions on page 28.

CONTINUED →

PREPARATION AND TIMING: To make this entire recipe in a day, carve out 4 to 5 hours. The chili itself takes up to 2 hours to cook. As it cools, make the dumpling dough and agar-agar water, and prep any additional fillings you plan to use. I usually make the chili and dough a day in advance, then refrigerate both until I'm ready to form and cook them.

FOR A THICKER FILLING: You can make this recipe as is, cool and chill it, and then form your dumplings, or you can add ½ cup cubed agar-agar water. Both ways are delicious, but I prefer the latter.

FOR A CHEESE-CONEY-WITH-EVERYTHING XLB DUMPLING: Fill each skin with 2 heaping teaspoons of the chili, ⅛ teaspoon onion, ¼ teaspoon cheese, ¼ teaspoon hot dog, 2 to 3 shakes of Frank's, and a dab of mustard.

CRAIN FAMILY CHILI

I've made my brother's Cincinnati chili recipe my own over the years—this is my slightly more spiced take on it. You'll find versions of this chocolate-and-cinnamon-laced ground beef chili in hundreds of chili parlors all over Cincinnati.

This recipe easily scales up; just add more simmer time and reduce the ratio of water to beef, since there will be less direct heat. For four pounds of beef, I use about two quarts of water.

Cincinnati chili goes well with oyster crackers—it's always served with them in parlors, so consider grabbing a bag. And former president Barack Obama and I both like the Cincinnati chili tradition of buying a York Peppermint Pattie at the parlor register to enjoy after the meal. Just so you know.

MAKES ABOUT 1 QUART

- 1 pound ground beef (10 to 15 percent fat, grass-fed if possible)
- 1 large yellow onion, pureed (about 1½ cups)
- 3 to 3½ cups water
- 2 to 3 tablespoons chili powder
- 1 to 2 teaspoons kosher salt
- 1½ teaspoons ground cinnamon
- ½ teaspoon ground cumin
- ¼ teaspoon ground allspice
- ¼ teaspoon garlic powder, or 2 cloves garlic, minced or pressed
- ¼ teaspoon ground cloves
- ⅛ to ¼ teaspoon cayenne
- ½ ounce unsweetened chocolate
- 2 bay leaves
- 1 cup tomato sauce
- 1 tablespoon cider vinegar (or whatever flavorful vinegar you want)
- 1½ teaspoons Worcestershire sauce
- 2 to 4 shakes red Tabasco sauce
- ½ cup agar-agar water (page 94; optional)

1 In a medium pot over high heat, add the ground beef, pureed onion, and 3 cups of the water, and bring to a boil. Reduce the heat to medium low and simmer for 30 minutes, uncovered, while breaking up the beef as much as possible and stirring occasionally.

2 In a small bowl, add the chili powder and salt to taste, cinnamon, cumin, allspice, garlic powder, cloves, and cayenne, and whisk to break up any clumps.

3 Add the spice mixture, chocolate, bay leaves, tomato sauce, vinegar, Worcestershire sauce, and Tabasco to the pot and stir to incorporate. Reduce the heat to low and simmer, uncovered, for 80 to 90 minutes, stirring occasionally. Add the remaining ½ cup water if necessary. You want the consistency of a moderately thick meat sauce or Bolognese. Set aside to cool to room temperature, and then refrigerate for at least 30 minutes (or up to 3 days). It freezes for up to 1 month.

4 Drain the agar-agar cubes if any water has sweated out, and add them to the chilled chili. Stir until they are evenly distributed.

NOTE: To make vegetarian black bean chili, soak ½ pound dried black beans overnight (12 or more hours). Drain and transfer to a medium pot, then add 4 to 4½ cups water and roughly half the amounts of all remaining ingredients (omitting the beef entirely, of course). Simmer, uncovered, for about 1½ hours, stirring occasionally, until the beans are fully cooked. Blend with an immersion blender to the consistency of a moderately thick soup.

CHILI ALL THE WAYS

If you are making this chili for three-ways (spaghetti, chili, cheese), four-ways (spaghetti, chili, cheese, and onion or bean), five-ways (spaghetti, chili, cheese, onion, *and* bean), or Coneys (hot dog in a bun with chili and cheese, and maybe onion and mustard), then I recommend upping the amount of water for a thinner chili, to get it to Cincinnati-chili-parlor consistency. Start by adding ½ cup more, but you'll probably ultimately add 1 cup water. Adjust the salt to taste, but all the other spices and seasonings should be good.

SHRIMP & GRITS

SOUTHERN US

SHAPE: XLB

COOK: Steam

SKIN: All-Purpose Egg Dough (page 42); do not use store-bought

GARNISH: The shrimp tail sticking out is all they need.

SAUCE: Sambal (page 152)

These dumplings incorporate one of my favorite family recipes— Garlic-Cheese Grits Casserole—with two things I also adore, shrimp and sambal. Serve these with Bananas Foster dumplings (page 129) for dessert. Both are yummy Southern dumplings that conjure up New Orleans. Sazerac, please!

Since these are a little tricky to form with the shrimp tail sticking out, I recommend using pliable homemade dumpling skins. (Or form them with the shrimp entirely inside the dumpling instead.) I encourage you to make my sambal, but if you use store-bought, add some lemon zest and finely grated fresh ginger to brighten it. If heat is an issue, a Cajun-spiced tomato sauce (made from stewed tomatoes, sautéed onion and garlic, and a Cajun spice blend) works well for dipping too.

MAKES 6 CUPS OF FILLING FOR 50 TO 60 DUMPLINGS

- × 1½ pounds All-Purpose Egg Dough
- × 4 cups Garlic-Cheese Grits Casserole (recipe follows)

- × ¼ cup homemade Sambal, or 2 to 3 tablespoons store-bought

- × 1 pound small (51/60-count) shrimp, peeled (see note)

CONTINUED

1 Prepare the dough according to the instructions on page 42. Do *not* use store-bought dumpling skins. Make 4-inch or larger skins to accommodate the shrimp.

2 Prepare the casserole according to the instructions below.

3 Fill the skins with 2 to 3 teaspoons of the cooled grits (break them up a bit so you get some of the cornflake-cheese mix in each), then ⅛ to ¼ teaspoon of sambal. Finally, push the shrimp into the grits, with the tail sticking up.

4 Form the dumpling around the shrimp tail according to the instructions for XLB on page 24 (shumai works too; see page 22).

5 Steam the dumplings according to the instructions on page 28.

NOTE: Store-bought sambal is often spicier than mine, so start with ⅛ teaspoon and incrementally adjust up.

Sometimes 51/60-count shrimp are hard to find, so if you use 41/50 or 36/40 size, cut off the top ½ inch or so of the shrimp and use those parts to fill the dumplings as well.

GARLIC-CHEESE GRITS CASSEROLE

I make this unbelievably tasty casserole with a hefty garlic kick a couple of times a year for holidays, and now you can too. I usually double the batch to double the likelihood of leftovers. It scales up perfectly, and there are *still* rarely any leftovers. Of all my recipes, this one, my homemade plum wine, and Crain Family Chili (page 122) are most requested from friends. Yes, there is a lot of butter in this casserole. And cheese, and milk, and eggs. It's Midwestern, like me. No apologies.

MAKES ABOUT 6 CUPS

- 4½ cups water
- 2 teaspoons kosher salt
- 1 cup grits or polenta
- 2 cups grated sharp cheddar cheese (about ¼ pound), divided
- 8 tablespoons (1 stick) unsalted butter, roughly chopped, divided
- 2 large eggs, whisked
- About ½ cup whole milk
- 8 cloves garlic, minced or pressed
- 1½ cups crushed cornflakes

1 Preheat the oven to 350 degrees F.

2 In a medium pot over high heat, bring the water and salt to a boil. Add the grits in a steady stream while whisking so that they don't clump. Return the grits to a boil, then reduce the heat to medium and simmer for 5 to 6 minutes, whisking regularly, until they have thickened and are bubbling and spitting with spite. And bite! (I often wear an oven mitt when whisking grits, and I also keep my body away from the pot because bubbling grits are painful if they get you.) They should be slightly undercooked at this point. If you are using very coarse stone-ground grits, cook them for 2 to 3 more minutes.

3 Remove the grits from the heat, and add 1½ cups of the cheese and 6 tablespoons of the butter. Stir until both have melted and fully incorporated.

4 Put the eggs in a 1-cup or larger measuring cup and add enough milk to equal 1 cup liquid. Whisk the milk and egg together to combine. Add this mixture and the garlic to the grits. Transfer the mixture into a 3- to 4-inch-deep 2-quart casserole dish.

5 In a small bowl, combine the cornflakes and the remaining ½ cup grated cheese. Spread them on top of the grits.

6 Melt the remaining 2 tablespoons butter, and drizzle it over the top of the casserole.

7 Bake for about 1 hour, until the grits are mostly set but still slightly jiggly. Set aside to cool for 10 to 15 minutes, and then serve warm if you are not making dumplings. If you are, cool the grits to room temperature, then cover and refrigerate them for at least 30 minutes before using as filling.

NOTE: You only need about 4 cups of the grits to fill the dumplings, but it's nice to have a bit left over. You can serve the extras in a mound in the middle of the dumpling platter, or slice and fry them up like polenta and serve them with eggs for breakfast.

BANANAS FOSTER *Vegetarian*

SOUTHERN US

SHAPE: Crescent

COOK: Pan-fry

SKIN: Cocoa All-Purpose Egg Dough (page 42)

GARNISH: Banana Liqueur (page 131)

SAUCE: Chocolatey Banana-Coconut (page 132)

My grandma Amy (RIP) had a lot of New Orleans recipes in her repertoire, and for dinner parties she loved to make her version of ignite-at-the-table bananas Foster, which was born in the kitchen of New Orleans' grande-dame restaurant Brennan's in 1951. Classic, dramatic, and full of character—just like her.

I cherished everything about the dessert—the caramelized, buttery bananas; the exciting torching and igniting of them right before serving; the way we all got a little tipple of rum with the bananas; and how everything swirled and melted together on the dessert plate. These dumplings are in honor of Amy. They're straight-up bananas Foster, just a pinch thicker and, well, in a dumpling. I highly recommend making cocoa skins for these.

MAKES 4½ TO 5 CUPS OF FILLING FOR 50 TO 60 DUMPLINGS

- 1½ pounds Cocoa All-Purpose Egg Dough, or 60 store-bought dumpling skins
- 6 tablespoons unsalted butter
- 1 cup light brown sugar
- ½ teaspoon kosher salt
- ½ teaspoon ground cinnamon
- 5 to 6 firm, medium-large ripe bananas, halved lengthwise and crosswise
- ⅓ cup Banana Liqueur (recipe follows) or crème de banane, plus more for serving
- ⅓ cup gold/amber or dark rum
- Vanilla or banana ice cream, for serving

CONTINUED

1 Prepare the dough according to the instructions on page 42, or set out the store-bought skins.

2 In a large skillet over medium-low heat, melt the butter, and then add the sugar, salt, and cinnamon. Cook for 2 to 3 minutes while stirring, breaking up any sugar clumps, until the sugar has mostly dissolved and the sauce has slightly thickened.

3 Add the bananas, increase the heat to medium high, and sauté for 4 to 5 minutes, flipping the bananas once, until they're light brown.

4 Remove from the heat. Add the liqueur and rum to the pan, and *do not* stir. Carefully ignite the bananas with a long-reach lighter and let the flame die out, about 1 minute.

5 With tongs or a spatula, remove the bananas from the pan, shaking the sauce off so that most of it remains in the pan, and put them on your cutting board.

6 Put the sauce-filled pan over medium-high heat and simmer for 1 to 2 minutes, stirring occasionally, to cook off the alcohol and thicken the sauce a bit. Remove from the heat.

7 Once the bananas are cool enough to handle, chop them. Once both the sauce and the bananas have cooled to room temperature, combine them and stir to incorporate. Cover and refrigerate for at least 30 minutes before using.

8 Form the dumplings according to the instructions on pages 44–46.

9 Pan-fry the dumplings according to the instructions on page 31.

10 Serve the dumplings on a platter surrounding scoops of vanilla ice cream (it will melt a bit from the warm dumplings) and drizzle everything with the banana liqueur.

NOTE: This is the perfect dessert to follow the Shrimp & Grits dumplings (page 125). Serve with small glasses of chilled Banana Liqueur.

To go all out, cook these and the Coconut-Sesame dumplings (page 89), and create a dumpling sundae topped with vanilla ice cream and drizzled with Chocolatey Banana-Coconut Sauce (page 132) and Banana Liqueur.

To make the dumplings vegan, use All-Purpose Eggless Dough (page 47) and a butter substitute. Serve with nondairy ice cream.

BANANA LIQUEUR

This super-flavorful liqueur blows me away every time I make it. I created it for the Bananas Foster dumplings because most commercial crème de banane is icky and expensive. This recipe is a really simple and delicious infusion. Slice a couple of bananas, bathe them in rum, wait several days, strain, and enjoy. Try it in a fantastic hot coconut coffee drink: in a small pot, warm one-quarter cup each banana liqueur and canned coconut milk for a few minutes while whisking, then combine with one-half cup freshly brewed hot coffee.

MAKES ABOUT 1 PINT

- 2 medium ripe bananas, sliced
- 1 cup light brown sugar
- 1 teaspoon vanilla extract
- 2 cups gold rum (I like Flor de Caña Añejo Oro)

1 Put the bananas, sugar, and vanilla into a quart jar.

2 Pour in the rum, gently stir to dissolve the sugar, and top with a lid. Let the liqueur sit at room temperature in a dark spot for 4 to 6 days, stirring it every day or so to move the darkening bananas around at the top. Taste it as you do!

3 Once it is banana flavored to your liking, remove the bananas and strain through a fine-mesh sieve lined with cheesecloth. Refrigerate for up to 2 months.

CHOCOLATEY BANANA-COCONUT SAUCE *Vegan*

Some of my favorite sweet-side-of-life things—dark chocolate, coconut, banana, and citrus—go into this sauce. And it's vegan (if you use vegan chocolate)! I especially love to drizzle this one over dumpling sundaes. When I was little, one of my babysitters made a healthy treat that I adored—toothpick-spiked banana segments that were dipped in lemon juice, rolled in wheat germ, and then frozen. I re-created them and tried them with this sauce, and it was so tasty.

MAKES ABOUT 1 CUP

- ½ cup semisweet chocolate chips or finely chopped semisweet chocolate (3 ounces)
- 1 ounce unsweetened chocolate, finely chopped
- ¾ cup canned coconut milk (stirred to combine the fat and milk)
- 2 tablespoons Banana Liqueur (page 131) or crème de banane
- 2 teaspoons finely grated lime zest (no pith; from about 1 medium lime)
- ⅛ teaspoon kosher salt

1 Put both chocolates in a medium heatproof bowl and set aside.

2 In a heavy-bottomed small pot over medium heat, add the coconut milk and bring to a simmer, whisking.

3 Remove from the heat, pour it over the chocolate, and let it stand without stirring for 2 to 3 minutes, until the chocolate has melted.

4 Whisk the sauce for 1 to 2 minutes, until glossy and smooth.

5 Add the liqueur, lime zest, and salt, and whisk to incorporate. Serve the sauce hot or at room temperature. Refrigerate for up to 1 week. To reheat, gently warm in a double boiler or heatproof bowl set over a pot, or cover and microwave in 15-second bursts, stirring between each round.

GOAT CHEESE ARRABBIATA *Vegetarian*

ITALY

SHAPE: Quenelle

COOK: Boil and bake

SKIN: Goat cheese batter

GARNISH: Parmesan cheese

SAUCE: Arrabbiata Sauce (page 137)

This book was born while I was eating these dumplings. I was at my cookbook collaborator and dear friend John Gorham's Tasty n Alder restaurant in Portland with a team from Sasquatch Books. That night we ordered all sorts of dishes, and the kitchen generously sent out ones that we didn't, including these crazy delicious, pillowy goat cheese dumplings nestled in *arrabbiata* sauce—the classic, spicy, Italian Lazio-region tomato sauce.

At that dinner, I told everyone how dumplings are one of my favorite foods, and how they are so fun to make. I was going on and on about my everlasting love when Sasquatch president Sarah Hanson looked at editorial director Jen Worick and said, "Are you thinking what I'm thinking? Liz, you should write a dumpling cookbook with us!" You know what my answer was.

MAKES ABOUT 12 MEDIUM DUMPLINGS FOR 3 TO 4 SERVINGS

- 5 cups Arrabbiata Sauce (recipe follows)
- 1 teaspoon kosher salt, plus more for boiling
- 3 large eggs
- ¼ cup heavy cream

- 3 tablespoons extra-virgin olive oil, divided
- 1 teaspoon freshly ground black pepper
- ½ teaspoon ground nutmeg

- 1 pound soft goat cheese (about 2 cups), room temperature
- 1 cup all-purpose flour
- ½ cup finely grated Parmesan cheese

CONTINUED

1   Prepare the arrabbiata sauce according to the instructions on page 137 before proceeding with the dumplings, up to 3 days in advance.

2   Fill a large pot three-quarters full with salted water and bring to a boil over high heat. If you want to cook all 12 dumplings at once, put two large pots of salted water to boil, but I advise using only one the first time you make these.

3   Meanwhile, in a large bowl, add the eggs, cream, 1 tablespoon of the olive oil, salt, pepper, and nutmeg, and whisk for 2 to 3 minutes, until everything is combined and beginning to froth.

4   Add the goat cheese, breaking it up with a large wooden spoon until incorporated. There will be some small lumps, but that's okay because you'll mix those in by hand in the next step.

5   Add the flour, stir a few times with a spatula, and then mix by hand or with the spatula to fully combine. Smash and blend in the goat cheese. This is a wet batter, so it will stick. After blending, there should be no streaks of goat cheese or flour. You can make the dumpling batter 2 to 3 days in advance and refrigerate it in an airtight container.

6   Line a baking sheet with parchment paper, and fill a medium bowl halfway with hot water. Dip one large spoon and one medium one in hot water, then shake off the excess. With the medium spoon, scoop up ¼ cup of the dumpling batter and form it into a quenelle (a tapered oblong, roundish shape) by turning the medium spoon around the dumpling in the larger spoon. Place it on the prepared baking sheet and continue with the remaining batter, dipping the spoons in the hot water between forming each dumpling. Batter will stick to the spoons no matter what, but hot water helps form and smooth the dumplings.

7   Before cooking the dumplings, check the water: you want a consistent, light simmer throughout cooking—never a full boil, or the dumplings will fall apart. Note that the water will become cloudy as bits of dumplings fall off, but don't worry about this. Gently transfer the dumplings to the simmering water in batches of no more than 6 at a time. Simmer for 6 to 7 minutes if the dumplings are room temperature, or 7 to 8 minutes if the batter has been refrigerated. Gently nudge them with a spoon several seconds after adding them to the pot so they don't stick to each other or the pot. After 2 to 3 minutes, they will float. Do not leave the stove while they cook. Remove them with a large slotted spoon, spider, or handled sieve onto a large plate.

8 Once all the dumplings are cooked, pour the hot arrabbiata sauce into a 9-by-13-inch casserole pan, and nestle the dumplings in it, leaving space between each. Drizzle them with the remaining 2 tablespoons olive oil.

9 Turn on the broiler and position an oven rack 6 to 8 inches below it.

10 Broil the dumplings for 3 to 4 minutes, until the tops have slightly browned. Remove them from the oven and test for doneness with a knife. If the insides are still wet and batterlike, continue to broil them for 2 to 3 more minutes, until the knife comes out clean.

11 Sprinkle the dumplings with the Parmesan right before serving.

NOTE: You can broil these dumplings in smaller batches, 3 dumplings per heaping cup of sauce. Evenly divide the olive oil and Parmesan and broil for slightly less time.

ARRABBIATA SAUCE

This is a Tasty n Alder version of the fiery, garlicky red sauce hailing from the Lazio region of Italy. The word *arrabbiata* actually means "angry" in Italian—referring to the sauce's biting heat. If you want to tame it a bit, simply use fewer chilies.

MAKES ABOUT 5 CUPS

- ¼ cup extra-virgin olive oil
- 3 to 4 tablespoons stemmed and minced oil-cured Calabrian chilies (12 to 16 chilies)
- 4 tablespoons minced or pressed garlic (about 1 head of garlic)
- 2 cups minced flat-leaf parsley leaves (about 2 bunches)
- 2 (28-ounce) cans whole peeled stewed tomatoes
- ½ to 1 teaspoon kosher salt
- ⅛ to ¼ teaspoon freshly ground pepper

1 In a medium pot over medium heat, cook the olive oil, chilies, and garlic for 4 to 5 minutes, until they begin to stick to the bottom of the pot and the garlic starts to turn golden.

2 Add the parsley and cook, stirring, for 1 minute, until wilted.

3 Break up the tomatoes by hand into small pieces, add them to the pot, and bring to a simmer.

4 Reduce the heat to medium low. Simmer the sauce, uncovered, for about 1½ hours, stirring occasionally, until the tomatoes have almost entirely broken down and the sauce has reduced by about a third. When the sauce is almost finished, use a large wooden spoon to break up any remaining tomato pieces. You want the sauce to be slightly chunky.

5 Season with the salt and pepper to taste and remove from the heat. Use right away or refrigerate for up to 2 days.

POTATO KOMPER

NORWAY

SHAPE: Ball

COOK: Simmer

SKIN: Potato and barley flour

GARNISH: Bacon and melted butter

SAUCE: None

Norwegian *komper* (pronounced KOOMP-er) are wintry, orange-sized, slow-simmered dumplings made of grated potato and barley flour and often filled with fatty salted meat. They are quite popular throughout Norway. There are *many* variations and other names for them, including *raspeballer*, *komler*, and *klubber*.

My friends Anders and Samantha, who live in Norway with their baby kompe (I mean, boy!), grew up eating komper often drizzled in butter and topped with crumbled bacon, sometimes sprinkled with sugar or dolloped with a spoonful of lingonberry jam or golden syrup.

According to Samantha, and I agree, komper leftovers are excellent for breakfast. "Slice them and fry them up in a pan with *lots* of butter." Just don't compress the komper too much before boiling, or you'll end up with the dreaded dense kompe. It's sort of like a floppy pickle. No one would wish this upon you.

MAKES 5 LARGE DUMPLINGS FOR 3 TO 4 SERVINGS

- 2¼ teaspoons kosher salt, divided, plus more for boiling
- ¼ pound fatty pork or lamb
- ⅛ plus ¼ teaspoon freshly ground black pepper, divided

- 1 cup all-purpose flour
- 1 cup barley flour
- ¼ teaspoon baking powder
- 2 pounds russet potatoes (about 3 large)

- ¼ cup (½ stick) unsalted butter, melted, for garnish
- ¼ pound bacon (3 to 4 slices), cooked and crumbled, for garnish

CONTINUED

1   Fill a large pot three-quarters full with salted water and bring to a boil over high heat.

2   Meanwhile, dice the meat. In a small bowl, mix it with ½ teaspoon of the salt (omit the salt if you are using ham) and ⅛ teaspoon of the pepper.

3   In a large bowl, mix the flours, the remaining 1¾ teaspoons salt, the remaining ¼ teaspoon pepper, and the baking powder.

4   Peel and grate the potatoes with a standard large-hole grater. If you have a food processor with a grating disc, you can use that, and roughly chop the potato after you have grated it into 1- to 2-inch pieces.

5   Wrap the grated potato in cheesecloth, a thin towel, or a nylon brewing bag. Over a large bowl, squeeze out as much potato water as possible—a few tablespoons or so. Set it aside for at least 2 minutes so that the potato starch settles. Carefully pour out and discard the potato water and keep the thick, pasty starch at the bottom. There should be 1 to 2 tablespoons of potato starch.

6   Add the grated potato and the potato starch (it is very dense and can be tough to remove; use a sturdy spatula or spoon) to the flour mixture. Mix by hand, squeezing and kneading the dough for 1 to 2 minutes, until it is well incorporated.

7   Fill one cupped hand with about ½ cup of dough and make a small indentation. Place a heaping tablespoon of the seasoned meat in it, and then cover the meat with about ½ cup more dough. Cup the dough with both hands and form it, by lightly squeezing and patting it, into an orange-sized dumpling roughly 3 inches in diameter. Be careful not to compress it too much—just enough so that it stays together and feels secure—or you'll end up with a dreaded dense komper.

8   Once the water is lightly boiling, gently place the komper in the pot one by one, carefully nudging them off the bottom. Lightly simmer for 45 to 50 minutes. Never go above a light simmer, or the komper will fall apart and you'll have potato soup. Every 5 minutes or so, give them a gentle nudge with a spoon so that they don't stick to the bottom of the pot or to one another. After 10 to 15 minutes, the komper will float. The cooking water will get a bit murky with dough and starch.

9   Remove the komper from the pot one by one with a large slotted spoon, spider, or handled sieve. Let the water fully drain off each. Drizzle with the melted butter and top with crumbled bacon and serve. Beware of eating more than one. They are heavy dumplings, suitable for a long hibernation.

NOTE: Pork belly or jowl, boneless pork or lamb rib meat, or ham will all work great for the filling.

To make the dumplings vegan, use vegetables, tempeh, or veggie sausage to fill and garnish the komper, as well as a butter substitute for the topping.

DUMPLINGS = LOVE

TO MAKE A TRADITIONAL MEAL: I like to boil a meaty smoked ham hock for 3 hours in a large pot filled three-quarters full with water. Then I remove the hock, add more water, and cook the komper. After cooking the komper, I return the hock to simmer for a few minutes, and serve it with the komper and boiled rutabaga mashed with butter, sour cream, and nutmeg.

IF THE KOMPER FALL APART: Simmer any komper that start to break apart in a handled sieve if possible. If they are too far gone for that, remove and finish cooking by sautéing in a covered pan over medium-low heat, with about 1 tablespoon of butter per komper, for roughly the remaining boil time, turning them occasionally.

SOUR PICKLE PIEROGI *Vegetarian*

EASTERN EUROPE

SHAPE: Crimped crescent

COOK: Boil and pan-fry

SKIN: All-purpose flour and sour cream

GARNISH: Sautéed onion, mustard, sauerkraut, and sour cream

SAUCE: Brown butter from the pan

Pierogi are typically savory, although sometimes sweet, potato- or meat-stuffed dumplings that can be baked, boiled, or pan-fried. Their exact origins are difficult to trace, but Russia, Poland, and the Ukraine all lay the most claims. The first time I had pierogi was at Portland's Polish Festival—a few years before I had the crazy-tasty from-scratch pierogi at my friends Vinny and Mel's Portland bar the Foggy Notion, which closed several years ago. My only addition to their recipe here, other than some minor tweaks, is diced sour pickle.

Give yourself plenty of time to make these. To divide and conquer, make the filling ahead of time and store it in the refrigerator, covered, for up to two days. After the dough has rested, wrap it in plastic wrap and refrigerate for up to two days. Remove it from the refrigerator one to two hours before rolling out the skins.

CONTINUED

MAKES 25 TO 30 MEDIUM PIEROGI FOR 3 TO 4 SERVINGS

FOR THE FILLING
× Kosher salt
× 1¼ pounds red potatoes (4 to 6 medium), peeled and cut into 2-inch cubes
× 1 tablespoon unsalted butter
× 1 tablespoon vegetable oil
× 1 cup finely diced yellow onion (about ½ small)
× Freshly ground black pepper

× ½ cup grated sharp cheddar cheese (about 1 ounce)
× ½ cup finely diced sour pickle (about 1 large pickle)

FOR THE DOUGH
× 2 cups all-purpose flour, plus more for dusting
× 1 tablespoon kosher salt, plus more for boiling

× 4 tablespoons (½ stick) cold unsalted butter, cut into ¼-inch cubes
× 1 large egg
× ½ cup sour cream

FOR SERVING
× ½ to ¾ cup (1 to 1½ sticks) unsalted butter
× 2 medium yellow onions, halved and sliced (about 4 cups)
× Dijon mustard, sour cream, and your favorite sauerkraut

MAKING THE FILLING

1 Fill a large pot three-quarters full with lightly salted water and bring to a boil over high heat. Add the potatoes and boil for about 15 minutes, until mashed-potato soft. Drain and set aside.

2 While the potatoes boil, in a medium skillet over medium-low heat, melt the butter and oil. Once the butter is bubbling, add the onions and a pinch of salt and pepper, and cook, stirring occasionally, until the onions are translucent and a bit caramelized. Cooking the onions should take about as long as boiling the potatoes, 15 minutes or so.

3 In a medium bowl, add the potatoes and onion (use a spatula to get all that pan butter and oil). Add a couple pinches each of salt and pepper. Mash the potatoes by hand. Once they are mashed-potato consistency, add the cheddar and stir until it is incorporated and melted. Add the pickle, stir, and set aside to cool.

NOTE: You can substitute up to ½ cup of a different finely diced pickled vegetable, such as kimchi, sauerkraut (squeeze out the moisture of both before adding), or pickled beets.

MAKING THE DOUGH

4 In the bowl of a stand mixer fitted with the hook attachment, add the flour and salt, and mix on medium-low speed (#2 on a KitchenAid) for 30 seconds.

5 Add the butter in a few batches, with the mixer still on medium-low speed, for 2 to 3 minutes per batch, until the butter is incorporated but still in small lumps.

6 Lock the head on the mixer and on medium speed (#4 on a KitchenAid), add the egg and sour cream, and mix for 3 to 4 minutes, until the dough forms a ball beside or around the hook.

7 Lightly dust your work surface with flour, turn out the dough, and knead it several times until smooth. Cover the dough with a damp towel, and put it under the inverted mixing bowl. Rest it for 30 minutes (up to 2 hours).

FORMING THE SKINS

8 Lightly dust your work surface with flour and roll out the dough, flipping it a few times, into a rounded rectangle a smidge less than ⅛ inch thick. Do not use a pasta machine for rolling this dough because it is too wet and will stick.

9 Use a 3- to 3½-inch round cookie cutter (Vinny, Mel, and I often use a 3½-inch cocktail shaker) to cut out the skins. Keep them lightly dusted with flour and separate enough so that they don't stick. Combine the leftover dough and roll it out up to two more times.

10 Lightly dust a platter with flour. Using your hands, form a 1- to 1½-inch-diameter ball (about 1 heaping tablespoon) of the cooled potato mixture, and place it in the middle of a pierogi skin. (Alternatively, form all the potato mixture into balls, place them on a baking sheet, and fill all pierogi at once.)

11 Hand-form the pierogi into a half circle by folding the skin over the ball and pulling the edges out a bit to pinch together. Push down on the potato-filled center slightly so it isn't too bulbous. This makes it easier to brown it evenly later.

12 Using the tines of a fork, crimp the rounded edge of the pierogi by lightly pressing down on the seam and then repeat on the other side. Place the formed pierogi on the prepared platter, making sure that none are touching.

CONTINUED >

BOILING THE DUMPLINGS

13 Fill a large pot three-quarters full with lightly salted water (or use two pots to cook them faster) and bring to a boil over high heat. Fill a large bowl with 3 cups ice and 1 quart cold water (make sure you have extra ice on hand). Line a platter with paper towels.

14 Boil the pierogi in batches of 6 to 8 for about 2 minutes each. (Use a small handled sieve to hold them in the boiling water if you have one.) Remove the pierogi from the water with a large slotted spoon, spider, or handled sieve, and place them in the ice bath for 1 to 2 minutes. Replace the ice as it melts.

15 Remove the pierogi from the ice bath and place them on the prepared platter. At this point, you can either carry on to the next step and pan-fry the pierogi, or remove the paper towel and keep them covered in the refrigerator, not touching, for up to 2 days.

PAN-FRYING & SERVING THE DUMPLINGS

16 Put a serving dish in the oven and preheat to warm.

17 In a large skillet over medium-low heat, melt 1 to 2 tablespoons of the butter until it starts to bubble. Add 6 to 8 pierogi with some space around each, and pan-fry for 5 to 6 minutes, flipping them two to three times, until golden brown. Make sure that every part gets golden brown, even the base. Prop them up next to one another to brown the bottoms. Add more butter if the pierogi stick or the pan gets dry.

18 Once they're golden brown, reduce the heat slightly and add about one-quarter to one-third (the former if you are cooking 6 and latter if you are cooking 8) of the onion. Cook the onion with the pierogi for about 10 minutes, until softened. Put the cooked pierogi and onion in the warm oven while cooking the remaining pierogi.

19 Serve immediately, pouring any remaining browned pan butter over the top of the pierogi. Serve with Dijon mustard, sour cream, and sauerkraut at the table.

SOUP IT UP

There are so many different tasty dumpling soups made around the world, such as hearty Korean *mandu-guk*, made with Pork & Kimchi Mandu (page 66); meaty and garlicky Russian *pelmeni* soup; Chinese wonton soup; German *Maultaschensuppe*, large dumplings loaded with meat; and Jewish *kreplach* in chicken soup. It's heartwarming that two of the world's most comforting foods—dumplings and soup—have made so many lasting holy matrimonies.

Dumpling soup is also a wonderful way to stretch a meal. Suddenly just twenty dumplings serve four to six hungry humans! Use any of the book's crescent or XLB-shaped dumplings for soup, and you can even fold and press the crescent ends into each other, like with tortellini, for reinforcement.

I usually make soup using frozen dumplings and a simple homemade dashi, which I often have on hand for miso soup or ramen. I warm up the dashi—one to two cups per person—and while it comes to a boil, I gather the other ingredients. I like to add miso, homemade ramen eggs, thinly sliced garlic chives or scallions, ribboned greens, dried wakame, kimchi (such as the Napa Kimchi on page 69), tempeh, and much more.

If an ingredient needs to be cooked, I'll place it in the pot with the dumplings (see page 34); otherwise, I simply top the soup with small mounds of everything (making sure it's all at room temperature) in a pretty way, much like the art of ramen bowls. If anything needs a quick flash in the pot to heat up, just use a large slotted spoon, spider, or han-dled sieve to give it a dunk.

Once the soup has been ladled and arranged, I often drizzle it with Chili Oil (page 150) or Sichuan Peppercorn Oil (page 159) before serving. If you don't have a handled serving tray, I highly recommend getting one. Serve dumpling soup to yourself or a loved one on a serving tray, eat with an Asian soup spoon and chopsticks, and suddenly all chins are up.

DIPPING SAUCES

A dumpling without a dipping sauce usually falls into two categories—a missed opportunity or a mucked-up to-go order. Dumplings are designed for sauce. For many folks, the art of mixing up their individual dumpling dipping sauces at the table is a well-honed ritual. A sauce's savory versus sweet, sour, and spicy notes sets the tone for the entire meal.

My go-to dumpling sauce tends toward this four-part combo, volume in descending order: soy sauce, vinegar (usually some of one of my homemade fruity vinegars), some heat (usually chili oil or sambal), and sesame oil. All the dipping sauces here are a breeze to make, and many can moonlight as stir-fry, fried rice, or noodle sauces. All keep for a good amount of time in the refrigerator and love to be taken for a spin on a lazy Susan.

CHILI OIL *Vegan*

I drizzle this oil on everything from noodle and ramen dishes (it's so tasty on ramen eggs!) to fish and fried rice. And, of course, I *love* it on dumplings and in dipping sauces. It's super easy to make, and when you do, it fills your home with its wonderful roasty-toasty aroma.

Play around with the dried chilies to find the perfect heat: add more or less and different types as you see fit.

MAKES ABOUT 1 CUP

- 6 to 10 dried arbol chilies, stemmed
- ¾ cup peanut or vegetable oil

- 5 cloves garlic, coarsely chopped
- 3 tablespoons unpeeled coarsely chopped fresh ginger

- ¼ cup toasted sesame oil
- ⅛ to ¼ cup red pepper flakes

1 In a medium skillet over medium-low heat, roast the whole arbol chilies for 3 to 4 minutes, shaking the pan and turning them occasionally, until they have bloomed (filling your kitchen with their sweet, spicy smell, lightly smoking, and probably making you cough a little) and slightly darkened. Leave the arbols whole.

2 In a small pot over medium-low heat, put the roasted arbols, peanut oil, garlic, and ginger. Bring the oil to a simmer, reduce the heat to low, and lightly simmer for 8 to 10 minutes, until a kitchen thermometer set in the oil reaches between 225 and 250 degrees F. The garlic will get golden and a bit crisped and brownish around the edges. Do not let it burn or your oil will have bitter notes.

3 Remove from the heat and cool for about 20 minutes. Pour the chili oil through a fine-mesh sieve into a wide-mouth half-pint or pint glass jar, or other nonreactive container. Discard the arbols, ginger, and garlic.

4 Return the strained oil to the small pot over medium-low heat, and stir in the sesame oil and pepper flakes. Bring the oil back to a simmer, and heat for 1 to 2 minutes, until a kitchen thermometer set in the oil reaches between 225 and 250 degrees F.

5 Cool at room temperature for 10 to 15 minutes, then transfer the chili oil to the glass jar (strain off the chili flakes if you want; I prefer to keep them in the oil). Cover the oil tightly with a lid, and store it in a cool place for up to 2 months.

A NOTE ABOUT HEAT

Arbol chilies can be found in the Latin or Mexican section in grocery stores, and their spiciness widely varies, so start with 6 and add more from there if you don't know how spicy yours are.

Also, I recommend adding 2 to 3 tablespoons whole Sichuan peppercorns, if you like them, in step 2. I also usually add ⅛ to ¼ cup coarse Korean red pepper flakes, a.k.a. *gochugaru*, along with the red pepper flakes in step 4. I especially like the grainy crunch, toasty flavor, mild heat, and brilliant red color that it adds.

SAMBAL *Vegan*

When there's a condiment in my life that I frequently buy, I want to learn how to make it. I love store-bought *sambal oelek*—a flavor-whop chili paste originally from Southeast Asia.

I'm proud of this recipe because it's so much better than any commercial sambal I've had. You can make it with any fresh hot chilies you like, although fleshy, medium to medium-hot chilies, such as cherry bombs or jalapeños, are best.

MAKES ABOUT 1 CUP

- 5 ounces red or green fresh (and fleshy) chilies, stemmed and coarsely chopped (about 1½ cups)
- 5 cloves garlic, coarsely chopped
- 1 (1-inch piece) peeled fresh ginger, coarsely chopped
- 1½ teaspoons sugar
- ¾ to 1 teaspoon kosher salt
- ½ cup water
- Freshly squeezed juice of ½ medium lemon (about 2 tablespoons)
- Finely grated zest of ½ medium lemon (about 1 tablespoon)
- 1½ tablespoons peanut or vegetable oil

1 In the bowl of a food processor or blender, combine the chilies, garlic, ginger, sugar, salt to taste, and water, and pulse 25 to 30 times, until pureed but still slightly chunky.

2 Transfer to a small pot over medium heat, bring to a boil, and then reduce the heat to medium low. Simmer for 10 to 12 minutes, stirring occasionally, until the chilies have softened.

3 Add the lemon juice, lemon zest, and oil, and cook for 2 to 3 more minutes, until incorporated. Remove from the heat. Cool to room temperature before serving. Refrigerate for up to 1 month.

NOTE: Remove the chili seeds only if you want to lessen the heat.

QUAIL EGG-STUFFED DUMPLINGS

Scotch eggs—the pub treat of a hard-boiled egg wrapped in sausage, breaded, and fried—have long been a favorite of mine, so I came up with a riff on them: a quail egg inside a dumpling! These work well with a tackier dumpling filling, such as Pork & Shrimp Shumai (page 75), Orange Chicken (page 73), or Salmon-Sesame (page 63).

Bring a pot of water to boil, and cook quail eggs for precisely 2 minutes for runny yolks, 3 minutes for soft yolks, and 4 minutes for hard-boiled. Cool the eggs in an ice bath and then carefully peel them.

Wet your hands and form about 1½ tablespoons of filling into a thin patty. Top it with a quail egg, gently wrap and pat the filling around the egg, and then place the "meatball" in a 4-inch dumpling skin. Form them as shumai or XLB, and then steam them (pan-frying will overcook the egg). Serve with one or more of the dumplings sliced down the center so that everyone can see the bonny quail egg inside.

SOY-LIME *Vegan*

I've been lucky enough to speak at the Tokyo Fermentation Future Forum in Japan twice, and after my first visit, I came home inspired and tried my hand at home-fermented shoyu (a.k.a. soy sauce) made from wheat berries and soybeans. It's so rich and full of deep umami. I mostly savor it, and let it shine, as a special finisher for dishes. I have, however, made this bright and super limey sauce with it. If you've never broken out of the mass-market soy sauce game, I recommend splurging on a nicer aged bottle. This sauce is so fresh and citrusy, it'll make you wink at whoever's close, even if you don't want to.

MAKES ABOUT 1 CUP

- ½ cup soy sauce
- ¼ cup freshly squeezed lime juice (from about 1 to 2 medium limes)
- 2 tablespoons mirin or dry sherry
- 1 tablespoon toasted sesame oil

- ½ to 1 teaspoon shichimi togarashi or nanami togarashi (or a pinch of cayenne plus ½ teaspoon toasted sesame seeds)

- 1 scallion (both white and green parts), thinly sliced

In a small bowl, combine the soy sauce, lime juice, mirin, oil, shichimi togarashi to taste, and scallion. Let sit at room temperature for at least 30 minutes before serving. Refrigerate for up to 1 week.

GYOZA *Vegan*

Some variation on this dipping sauce is my usual go-to for Asian dumplings. I love how bright and complex it is, and how yummy it is in stir-fries, rice dishes, soups, fresh dumpling skin noodles, and more. If no one is looking, I might just take a sip from the gyoza sauce bowl to whet my whistle. It's deeply comforting.

Japanese gyoza sauce usually includes soy sauce, rice vinegar, and chili oil. Sometimes it's heavier on the rice vinegar, the way Gabe and Kana of Giraffe (see page 87) prefer it. I lean more toward soy sauce with this one.

MAKES ABOUT 1 CUP

- ½ cup plus 2 tablespoons soy sauce
- ¼ cup plus 2 tablespoons rice vinegar
- 2 teaspoons Chili Oil (page 150) or *rayu* (a.k.a. *layu*) or another store-bought chili oil
- 1 teaspoon toasted sesame oil
- ½ teaspoon sugar
- 1 scallion (both white and green parts), thinly sliced

In a small bowl, combine the soy sauce, vinegar, oils, sugar, and scallion. Stir to dissolve the sugar, and let it sit for at least 30 minutes at room temperature before serving. Refrigerate for up to 1 week.

SESAME-LIME

GINGERY SOY-LEMON

SAMBAL

GYOZA

CITRUSY SAMBAL-SOUR CREAM

CHILI OIL

PEANUT-CHILI

SOY-LIME

SICHUAN PEPPERCORN OIL

SESAME-LIME *Vegan*

This sauce is fantastic with seafood, especially the Salmon-Sesame dumplings (page 63), because it has some sweetness balanced by a subtly complex bitterness and a good amount of bright citrus. It's also super delicious hot or cold on noodles—including *dan dan* noodles (see page 161), udon, and soba—and falafel. The yield is just right for about one pound of noodles.

MAKES ABOUT 1 CUP

- ½ cup water
- ⅓ cup plus 2 tablespoons sesame paste or tahini, with some of its oil
- 1 to 2 tablespoons Sambal (page 152), or 1 tablespoon store-bought

- Freshly squeezed juice of ½ medium lime (about 1½ tablespoons)
- Finely grated zest of ½ medium lime (about 1 teaspoon)
- 1 tablespoon toasted sesame oil
- 1 teaspoon sugar

- ½ to 1 teaspoon kosher salt
- 1 (1-inch) piece peeled fresh ginger, coarsely chopped
- 1 scallion (both white and green parts), thinly sliced

In the bowl of a food processor or blender, combine the water, sesame paste, sambal, lime juice and zest, oil, sugar, salt to taste, and ginger. Puree for 20 to 30 seconds, until smooth. Stir in the scallions. (Alternatively, you can mince or grate the ginger and whisk everything in a medium bowl for 1 to 2 minutes, until combined.) Let sit for at least 30 minutes before serving. Refrigerate for up to 1 week.

NOTE: Store-bought sambal is often spicier than mine, so start with 1 tablespoon and incrementally adjust up.

SICHUAN PEPPERCORN OIL *Vegan*

One of the many things working on this book opened up to me is cooking with Sichuan peppercorn. Before this, I'd only ever eaten it in stir-fries, mapo tofu, and noodle dishes at restaurants. It turns out I love these powerful little numbing pods. My favorite way to use them is in this oil (or added to the Chili Oil on page 150) because it distributes their flavor and numbing effect and keeps for a very long time. Drizzle this oil over everything from noodles, soups, and shellfish to sautéed greens and fried rice.

MAKES ABOUT 1 CUP

× ¼ cup whole Sichuan peppercorns

× ¾ cup peanut or vegetable oil

× ¼ cup toasted sesame oil

1 In a medium pan over medium-low heat, roast the peppercorns for 2 to 3 minutes, shaking them a few times in the pan, until they release their fragrance.

2 In a small pot over medium-low heat, cook the roasted peppercorns and peanut oil until they come to a light simmer. Simmer for 2 to 3 minutes, until a kitchen thermometer set in the oil reaches between 200 and 225 degrees F.

3 Remove the peppercorn oil from the heat, stir in the sesame oil, and let the oil steep for about 30 minutes. Pour the oil through a fine-mesh sieve into a half-pint glass jar or other nonreactive container, and discard the peppercorns. Cover tightly with a lid and keep in a cool place for up to 2 months.

CITRUSY SAMBAL– SOUR CREAM *Vegetarian*

Think of this as a cooling sauce with some kick to dunk seafood and meaty dumplings in. If the dumpling has lime in it, use lime juice here; ditto for lemon. Make this into a chip dip by simply halving or quartering the sambal, adding two to three teaspoons of an herb or spice blend like chili powder or Cajun or ranch seasoning, and topping it with finely chopped chives or scallions. It's also *really* good with a generous swirl of Chili Oil (page 150).

MAKES ABOUT 1 CUP

- ½ cup plus 2 tablespoons sour cream
- 2 to 3 tablespoons Sambal (page 152), or 1 tablespoon store-bought
- 2 tablespoons cold water
- Freshly squeezed juice of ½ medium lime (about 1½ tablespoons) or ½ medium lemon (about 2 tablespoons)
- Finely grated zest of ½ medium lime (about 1 teaspoon) or lemon (about 1 tablespoon)
- ⅛ to ¼ teaspoon kosher salt
- Pinch to ⅛ teaspoon freshly ground black pepper

In a small bowl, add the sour cream, sambal, water, citrus juice and zest, and salt and pepper to taste. Whisk together until fully combined, and refrigerate for at least 30 minutes before serving. Refrigerate for up to 3 to 4 days.

NOTE: Store-bought sambal is often spicier than mine, so start with 1 tablespoon and incrementally adjust up.

PEANUT-CHILI *Vegan*

Beyond being a great sauce for dumplings, veggies, and salad rolls, this sauce is fantastic with noodles. For that, simply add a bit more peanut butter and oil to thicken it and make it silkier. For quick and easy Sichuan dan dan noodles, use this sauce or Sesame-Lime (page 158). Both are so good in it.

To make dan dan noodles, boil one pound of udon or other Asian wheat noodles according to the package instructions; brown half a pound of ground pork; and mix the noodles, this sauce, and the pork along with Chili Oil (page 150) or Sichuan Peppercorn Oil (page 159), sesame seeds, garlic chives or scallions, and roasted and chopped peanuts.

MAKES ABOUT 1 CUP

- ⅓ cup plus 2 tablespoons smooth peanut butter
- 3 tablespoons toasted sesame oil
- 3 tablespoons freshly squeezed lime juice (from 1 medium lime)
- 3 tablespoons cold water
- 1 to 2 tablespoons Sambal (page 152), or 1 tablespoon store-bought
- 2 tablespoons soy sauce
- 1 tablespoon sugar
- 1 (1-inch) piece peeled fresh ginger, chopped

In the bowl of a food processor or blender, combine the peanut butter, oil, lime juice, water, sambal, soy sauce, sugar, and ginger. Puree for 20 to 30 seconds, until smooth. (Alternatively, you can mince or grate the ginger and whisk everything in a medium bowl for 1 to 2 minutes, until combined.) Refrigerate for up to 1 week.

NOTE: Store-bought sambal is often spicier than mine, so start with 1 tablespoon and incrementally adjust up.

DUMPLING PARTY

My party philosophy has evolved over the years. I used to spend most of my time at every party I threw, no matter the size, tied to the kitchen, making things for my guests, particularly cocktails. Though I enjoyed that, I ultimately realized I wanted to focus on my loved ones rather than the tasks. For a dumpling party, most of the work can be done ahead of time, allowing you to simply set a kitchen timer for round after round of dumpling fun.

The eighth wonder of the world *might* just be a rainbow of dumplings in a party-sized array of bamboo steamers, surrounded by dipping sauces. And plenty of chopsticks! Lucky for you, this is easy to pull off. Make a few types of dumplings ahead of time with colorful, flavorful skins (see page 52); freeze and label them; and when your freezer is full, it's party time! Plan for about ten dumplings plus a small side dish (steamed rice, kimchi, sautéed greens) per person. If you don't have a lazy Susan for serving, consider getting one.

Figure out ahead of time how you'll cook the frozen dumplings, and in what order. I usually start with a couple rounds of steamed, then move into pan-fried and boiled. After several rounds of dumpling deliciousness (often with a nice long walk or some dancing in between), I put an enormous dessert dumpling sundae (see note on page 130) in the middle of the table for everyone to share.

Another type of dumpling party is BYOF—bring your own filling, where everyone makes dumplings together. Be sure to clear plenty of work space in the kitchen; arrange for folks to make dumpling fillings ahead of time or bring ingredients the day of, including agar-agar cubes (see page 94) if you're making XLB; provide plenty of filling spreaders; and either make several colorful dumpling doughs pre-party and refrigerate or freeze them (see page 3), or set out the store-bought skins. Clear freezer room ahead of time so that you can freeze dumplings in batches for folks to take home.

GINGERY SOY-LEMON *Vegan*

The interplay of the two rich and dark ferments here—soy sauce and black vinegar—with the bright ginger and lemon is striking. This no-heat sauce, in both senses of *heat*, goes very well with many of this book's dumplings, particularly the Orange Chicken (page 73), because it's so nicely balanced. You get years of flavor in every dunk with this inky, addictive dipping sauce—sour, salty, savory, bitter, *and* sweet.

MAKES ABOUT 1 CUP

- ¼ cup plus 2 tablespoons soy sauce
- ¼ cup black vinegar
- 3 tablespoons water

- Freshly squeezed juice of ¼ medium lemon (about 1 tablespoon)

- 1 (1-inch) piece peeled fresh ginger, julienned

In a small bowl combine the soy sauce, vinegar, water, lemon juice, and ginger, and let it sit for at least 30 minutes at room temperature before serving. Refrigerate for up to 2 weeks.

ACKNOWLEDGMENTS

Working on this book has been a dream come true from start to finish, and there are a lot of people who've made it so. First, thank you to all the bright and shining stars at Sasquatch Books. Sasquatch also published my first book (*Food Lover's Guide to Portland*) and my third book (*Hello! My Name Is Tasty*). They are one of my closest publishing families. Thank you in particular to Gary Luke, my first editor at Sasquatch and their publisher extraordinaire for twenty-five years until his recent retirement; president Sarah Hanson and editorial director Jen Worick, who are responsible for the original idea for this book; executive editor Susan Roxborough; designer Tony Ong; art director Anna Goldstein; project editor Rachelle Longé McGhee; and copy editor Kirsten Colton. I love you all so much.

Thank you to my kick-ass editorial and recipe-testing assistant, Emily Park. You brought so much wisdom and organization to this project. I'm really glad we got to test some recipes together too. Speaking of that, thank you to the fabulous twenty-plus recipe testers across the country who helped make these recipes foolproof: Brian Bushaw and Beth Zinsli; Jim Carmin; Jen Datka; Lena Davidson; Carmelita Dominguez; Amy Fields; Anthony Green and Anna Swenson; Ellie Haimsohn; Rebecca Koon; Glen Lawrence and Stephanie Foyer; Lola Milholland; Theresa Minor, Jake Tinsley, and Judy Tinsley;

Radhika Natarajan; Cordelia Newbury; Beth Ransick; Cindy Ross; Kevin Scullin; Kyoko and Shiori Shinohara; Abby Seemann; Dana and Oliver Sturtevant; and finally, Veronica Vichit-Vadakan, who became a *Jeopardy!* champion during editing of the book! I am so very grateful to all of you for your generosity and excellent feedback.

Pauline Theriault at Multnomah County Library—thank you for helping me with food-research projects, including my shoyu and doubanjiang research, especially for this cookbook. You opened so many research doors to me (literally, I explored the cavernous stacks below Central!), and the book wouldn't be as rich and storied as it is without you.

I could not be happier with the photos throughout these pages. Thank you heaps and heaps to photographer Dina Avila and food stylist Nathan Carrabba for making all of my dumplings come to life. At my house! I love that we shot at my house and in my kitchen.

Thank you to Sou'wester Arts, in Seaview, Washington, particularly owner Thandi Rosenbaum, for giving me solo space and time to create (and a sauna to steam myself *without* my dumplings!) and write and edit this book. Thank you to the biker women from BC who stayed next to me in the African Queen while I finished the book. You wild ones know how to live.

Thanks to all my friends and family for your love and support, always and forever. Thank you, Raquel, for being my dumpling-making queen for life. Thank you to my nieces Hannah and Marielle for being my favorite dumpling co-chefs. Thank you to Loly and Lil Jasper for being my sweetest recipe-testing dumpling-train stop—choo choo! I'm so glad Jaspie's first dumpling was this book's Pork XLB. Thank you to Michelle and Kylie for always being up for a dumpling party. Thank you to my loving housemate, Michelle, who put up with a freezer perpetually overfilling with dumplings and me being in the kitchen even more than usual for months. Thank you to my sweet malamute shepherd, Rubin, a.k.a. the White Wolf, for rocking the kitchen-floor-cleaning detail during recipe development and testing.

I'd like to thank some of my many food heroes, living and RIP, for paving the way, particularly Sandor Ellix Katz, Mark Bittman, Julia Child, Jacques Pépin, Nigel Slater, M. F. K. Fisher, and Anthony Bourdain.

Thank you to my agent, Kimberly Witherspoon, who I'll always pinch myself over getting to work with.

Thank you to all the culinary cultures worldwide, particularly throughout China, and the people who build those cultures, for hand-forming, steaming, frying, and boiling countless delicious dumplings from time immemorial.

Finally, thank you to my finest of fellows, Jimbo, who put up with a fair few *Dumplings Equal Love* meltdowns, particularly during the final stretch of recipe testing, when a tennis injury wounded my wing and severely fractured my confidence. Thank you, my love. In the sequel to this book I'll be sure to include a fuzzy peach dumpling in your honor. And kiss it.

FURTHER READING

Whenever I want to dig deep into a culinary culture, I hit the books. For *Dumplings Equal Love*, I spent a lot of time with my friend and Multnomah County Library research librarian Pauline Theriault, hunting and gathering books and digital database files that informed me on everything from the Sichuan ferment *doubanjiang*, and how it has historically been key for mapo tofu, to the history of imperial Chinese dumplings and the banquets at which they were served.

A lot of the books I spent time with were not translated into English, and that was intentional. There are many ways to gather information and learn, and those books, in particular, provided visual information via regional cuisine, techniques and processes, presentation, and overall cultural context.

I even got to delve into the belly of the beast to peruse downtown Portland's Central Library stacks. Many of the books that informed me deeply during the research and development of these recipes are older than I am, and many are out of print. If you have a hard time finding any of them, please know that the public library system is your friend, and more likely than not you can access some sort of interlibrary loan, usually a free service, to acquire them from a wide network of participating libraries. I highly recommend tapping into that service.

Chu, Grace Zia. *Madame Chu's Chinese Cooking School*. New York: Simon & Schuster, 1975.

Grace Zia Chu taught Americans how to cook Chinese food for decades, and this book is loaded with her stories, tasty recipes, and heaps of info about China and its food.

Editors of *China Pictorial*. *Chinese Cuisine from the Master Chefs of China*. Boston: Little Brown and Company, 1983.

A deeply informative cookbook focused on regional Chinese food and cuisine that features sixteen of China's master chefs (most of whom kicked off cooking careers at fourteen years old or younger) and their preparations of everything from sea slugs and shark's fin to cliff-swallow nests.

Kwak, Jenny. *Dok Suni: Recipes from My Mother's Korean Kitchen*. New York: St. Martin's Press, 1998.

This heartfelt cookbook comes from the mother-daughter duo of the since-closed namesake NYC restaurant. From the introduction: "The phrase [Dok Suni] describes a strong woman of any age, resilient and fearless. A woman of endurance. I realized that this was how my mother perceived herself. And since that day, my views on what it means to be my mother's daughter changed entirely."

Lee, Edward. *Buttermilk Graffiti: A Chef's Journey to Discover America's New Melting-Pot Cuisine*. New York: Artisan, 2018.

This was my favorite book of 2018. It flips the script from origin-erasing culinary appropriation to Lee's mission of deep cultural understanding and appreciation.

Leung, Mai. *The New Classic Chinese Cookbook*, 2nd ed. Tulsa, OK: Council Oak Books, 1998.

There are two hundred delicious recipes—originating from Sichuan and Hunan to Beijing and eastern and southern China—and deeply personal stories to go with them in this beautiful book, which was first published in 1976.

Leung, Mai. *Dim Sum and Other Chinese Street Food*. New York: Harper Colophon Books, 1982.

This Mai Leung cookbook was my well-worn gateway to dim sum culture, history, and recipes. Leung's generous stories and research plus all the beautiful hand-drawn illustrations throughout the book by Claude Martinot make it an absolute keepsake.

Lin, Florence. *Florence Lin's Complete Book of Chinese Noodles, Dumplings, and Breads*. New York: William Morrow & Company, 1986.

I am forever grateful to Florence Lin (RIP) for her generosity in teaching Chinese cuisine through her classes and cookbooks. A deeply moving and informative education in Chinese cuisine can be had simply by spending time with a stack of her books—this one was my introduction to the wide world of Chinese dumplings.

Ling, Kong Foong. *The Food of Asia: Fabulous Recipes from Every Corner of Asia*. Singapore: Periplus Editions Ltd., 2002.

Equal parts cookbook and history lesson, *The Food of Asia* has taught me so much, particularly about imperial Chinese banquet foods. It includes an A-to-Z ingredients section that is especially valuable.

Nguyen, Andrea. *Asian Dumplings: Mastering Gyoza, Spring Rolls, Samosas, and More.* Berkeley: Ten Speed Press, 2009.

Andrea Nguyen is a food hero of mine—I learned all about Vietnamese food from her books. This comprehensive cookbook includes more than seventy-five recipes for yummy Asian "hidden" foods, including dumplings.

Perkins, David W., ed. *Hong Kong and China Gas Chinese Cookbook.* Hong Kong: Hong Kong Pat Printer, 1978.

Hong Kong and China Gas Co. was formed in London in the mid-1800s and served as Hong Kong's first public utility company. The company hosted cooking lessons for decades, and this compendium of the recipes contains an introduction to Chinese food, culinary history, philosophies of eating, and much more.

Schafer, Charles and Violet. *Wokcraft.* San Francisco: Yerba Buena Press, 1972.

This cookbook, which is full of character, was produced by a husband-and-wife duo as a love letter to Chinese food that stemmed from Charles's two tours of duty in China as a young man. The recipes are fairly basic, but the stories are generously detailed and well told.

Simonds, Nina. *Classic Chinese Cuisine.* Boston: Houghton Mifflin, 1982.

Simonds's *Gourmet* magazine column about being an American chef-in-training in Taiwan led to this cookbook loaded with inspired recipes, stories, and detailed accounts of regional culinary customs.

Steinberg, Rafael. *The Cooking of Japan.* New York: Time-Life Books, 1969.

I appreciate this Time-Life series edition for its focus on the 1960s expansion of American cuisine. It includes instructions on making Japanese staples such as dashi as well as a lot of Japanese menu planning.

Tropp, Barbara. *The Modern Art of Chinese Cooking: Techniques and Recipes.* New York: William Morrow, 1982.

From the author's note, which I love: "Perhaps most of all, this book is my mirror. It is not a comprehensive record of a civilization or an encyclopedia of a cuisine, but rather the reflection of one person's studies, taste, vision, and style, and of a life that is lived happily between East and West." The recipes are fantastic too.

Tsuji, Shizuo. *Japanese Cooking: A Simple Art.* Tokyo; New York: Kodansha USA, 1980.

A classic, must-have Japanese cookbook for anyone who wants to dig deep into the cuisine and culture.

Wu, Sylvia. *Madame Wu's Art of Chinese Cooking.* Los Angeles: Bantam Books, 1973.

This sturdy little book is a touching personal account of growing up into the wide world of Chinese cuisine and making a life out of teaching Chinese cooking classes and writing cookbooks, along with a wonderful story about jade chopsticks and learning how to not lose your temper.

INDEX

Note: Page numbers in *italic* refer to photographs.

Printed in China

SASQUATCH BOOKS with colophon is a registered trademark of Penguin Random House LLC

24 23 22 21 20   9 8 7 6 5 4 3 2 1

Editors: Susan Roxborough and Jen Worick
Production editor: Rachelle Longé McGhee
Photographer: Dina Avila
Designer: Tony Ong
Food and prop styling: Nathan Carrabba

Library of Congress Cataloging-in-Publication Data

Names: Crain, Liz, author.
Title: Dumplings = love : delicious recipes from around the world / Liz
  Crain.
Other titles: Dumplings equal love
Description: Seattle : Sasquatch Books, [2020] | Includes bibliographical
  references and index. | Summary: "A single-subject cookbook featuring a
  collection of 45-50 dumpling recipes from around the world"— Provided
  by publisher.
Identifiers: LCCN 2019052781 (print) | LCCN 2019052782 (ebook) | ISBN
  9781632172969 (hardcover) | ISBN 9781632172976 (ebook)
Subjects: LCSH: Dumplings. | International cooking.
Classification: LCC TX769 .C69 2020 (print) | LCC TX769 (ebook) | DDC
  641.81/5—dc23
LC record available at https://lccn.loc.gov/2019052781
LC ebook record available at https://lccn.loc.gov/2019052782

ISBN: 978-1-63217-296-9

Sasquatch Books
1904 Third Avenue, Suite 710
Seattle, WA 98101

SasquatchBooks.com

CONVERSIONS

VOLUME

UNITED STATES	METRIC	IMPERIAL
¼ tsp.	1.25 mL	
½ tsp.	2.5 mL	
1 tsp.	5 mL	
½ Tbsp.	7.5 mL	
1 Tbsp.	15 mL	
⅛ c.	30 mL	1 fl. oz.
¼ c.	60 mL	2 fl. oz.
⅓ c.	80 mL	2.5 fl. oz.
½ c.	120 mL	4 fl. oz.
1 c.	230 mL	8 fl. oz.
2 c. (1 pt.)	460 mL	16 fl. oz.
1 qt.	1 L	32 fl. oz.

LENGTH

UNITED STATES	METRIC
⅛ in.	3 mm
¼ in.	6 mm
½ in.	1.25 cm
1 in.	2.5 cm
1 ft.	30 cm

WEIGHT

AVOIRDUPOIS	METRIC
¼ oz.	7 g
½ oz.	15 g
1 oz.	30 g
2 oz.	60 g
3 oz.	90 g
4 oz.	115 g
5 oz.	150 g
6 oz.	175 g
7 oz.	200 g
8 oz. (½ lb.)	225 g
9 oz.	250 g
10 oz.	300 g
11 oz.	325 g
12 oz.	350 g
13 oz.	375 g
14 oz.	400 g
15 oz.	425 g
16 oz. (1 lb.)	450 g
1½ lb.	750 g
2 lb.	900 g
2¼ lb.	1 kg
3 lb.	1.4 kg
4 lb.	1.8 kg

TEMPERATURE

OVEN MARK	FAHRENHEIT	CELSIUS	GAS
Very cool	250–275	120–135	½–1
Cool	300	150	2
Warm	325	165	3
Moderate	350	175	4
Moderately hot	375	190	5
Fairly hot	400	200	6
Hot	425	220	7
Very hot	450	230	8
Very hot	475	245	9

For ease of use, conversions have been rounded.